BEL

# BELIEVE THE GOOD NEWS

## Teacher's Book

SHEILA KIRWAN
LINDA P. GARLAND

GILL AND MACMILLAN

Published in Ireland by
Gill and Macmillan Ltd
Goldenbridge
Dublin 8
with associated companies throughout the world
© Linda P. Garland and Sheila Kirwan, 1990
0 7171 1851 7
Print origination in Ireland by
Design Image, Dublin
and
Criterion Press Ltd, Dublin


Nihil Obstat
Oliver V. Brennan B.D., M.A.
Imprimatur
✠ Tomás Cardinal Ó Fiaich, Archbishop of Armagh
6 May 1990

All rights reserved. No part of this publication may be copied, reproduced or
transmitted in any form or by any means, without permission of the publishers.
Photocopying any part of this book is illegal.

# CONTENTS

**Foreword** vii

**Part I: Introduction** 1
Religious Education 1
Planning Your Religious Education Programme 5
Education in Personal Development 7
Teaching Through Drama 16
Guide to Terms: Pupil Text 18
Guide to Terms: Teacher's Book 22

**Part II: Classwork** 23
Unit I: Stewardship of God's Creation 24
Chapter 1: Me 24
    2: Story 26
    3: My World 27
    4: I am Created in God's Image 29
    5: My Response to God's Creation 30
    6: How Free Am I? 30
    7: Meeting God 33
    8: Free to Choose 34
    9: Making Decisions 35

Unit II: Relationships 36
Chapter 10: Adolescence 36
    11: Growing Up 38
    12: Family 38
    13: Friendship 39
    14: God's Call and My Response 41
    15: Being a Steward to Myself 42

Unit III: Relationships in Trouble 42
Chapter 16: Sin 42
    17: The Breakdown of Relationships 43
    18: Rebuilding Broken Relationships 44
    19: Evil and Suffering 45
    20: Death and Eternal Life 46

Unit IV: Scripture 47
Chapter 21: The History of Salvation 47
    22: Exodus 48
    23: The Gospels 49
    24: Jesus 50

|  | 25: | Images of Jesus | 50 |
|---|---|---|---|
|  | 26: | Jesus' Death and Resurrection | 51 |

| Unit V: Sacraments | | | 52 |
|---|---|---|---|
| Chapter 27: | Signs and Symbols | | 52 |
| 28: | The Presence of Jesus | | 53 |
| 29: | Reconciliation | | 54 |
| 30: | The Eucharist | | 55 |
| 31: | The Sacrament of the Sick | | 56 |

| Unit VI: The Christian Community | | 57 |
|---|---|---|
| 32: | The Church — Called to Serve | 57 |
| 33: | Some Christian Denominations | 58 |
| 34: | The Orthodox Church | 58 |
| 35: | Christian Unity | 59 |

| Unit VII: The Liturgical Year | | 60 |
|---|---|---|
| Chapter 36: | Advent | 60 |
| 37: | Christmas | 60 |
| 38: | Lent | 61 |
| 39: | Easter | 62 |
| 40: | Pentecost | 63 |

| Unit VIII: Worship and Prayer | | 64 |
|---|---|---|
| 41: | Mary | 64 |
| 42: | Prayer | 65 |
| 43: | Prayer in the Life of Jesus | 65 |

# FOREWORD

If religious education is to be effective, we must succeed in linking the life experience of our pupils with faith statements. It is not enough to have the correct message: we must find a way of communicating the Christian message so that it can be heard. Young people must know that the Christian message is about them and their lives. If the adolescents of our time are going to become people of real faith, then they must be helped to see that religion and life are inextricably intertwined.

The authors of *Believe the Good News,* the second book of 'The Light of the World' series, have very successfully created a religion text which will enable the catechist to teach in a way that young adolescents will know that religion is relevant to their everyday lives. In other words, pupils will be enabled not only to know about God, but to know God; not only to know about Jesus and his message, but to discover the truth of his message in their lives; not just to know about the Church, but to feel that they are the Church. The text is designed to help students look more deeply at their experience and to challenge them with the Christian message relevant to that experience.

Perhaps the most obvious characteristic of *Believe the Good News* is that it comes from the hands of teachers who are in the classroom each day. It is down-to-earth, practical and usable by any teacher of religion, specialist or non-specialist. Furthermore, this religious education programme is created in a way which will allow for its use with pupils of all levels of ability.

Linda Garland and Sheila Kirwan are making a very significant contribution towards the catechesis of young adolescents through the writing of 'The Light of the World' series. I wish them every success in developing Book 3 of this new Junior Cycle Religious Education Programme.

Reverend Oliver Brennan

# PART I  INTRODUCTION

*Believe the Good News* is designed to help the religion teacher to plan and carry out an effective programme of religious education for 13 to 14-year-old students. The textbook is based on an experiential approach to teaching and takes as its starting point the needs and experiences of students.

*Believe the Good News* is the second textbook in 'The Light of the World' series. It builds upon and develops the concepts, ideas and doctrines introduced in *A New Commandment*, the first book of the series.

Each chapter provides 'starter' material, which the teacher can use to help students explore some important aspects of their experience. It also contains the Christian message directly relevant to those experiences, in a form readily understood by students of most levels of ability. Finally, each chapter gives suggestions as to how students might apply the Christian message to their own lives, or put it into practice.

'The Light of the World' series covers all topics outlined in the National Syllabus for Religious Education in the junior cycle. It provides further material relating to the Liturgical Year, the Sacraments, the Christian community, Prayer and Personal Development. In *Believe the Good News*, the themes of Personal Development, Relationships, God's love for us and our response to that love are explored in the context of experiences common to 13- and 14-year-olds. The more important of these include the experiences of wonder and challenge, growth and change, greater responsibility and freedom, limitations and frustrations, the need to love and be loved, to be special, to be healed and reconciled, to celebrate and give thanks, to know and understand.

## RELIGIOUS EDUCATION

The experiential approach to religious education adopted in this series reflects the authors' experience in the classroom. Students remember and can apply to their own lives the Christian doctrine which is directly relevant to their own experience and which is presented in a language they can understand.

*Some basic principles*
This approach is based on the following principles:
1. Religious education means educating people about themselves at the deepest possible level:
   — facilitating personal exploration and discovery.
   — teaching the skills necessary for such exploration (analysis, evaluation, etc.).
   — encouraging personal development of the whole individual in the context of the community.
2. Religious education means enabling students to see the presence of God within themselves and in the life of the community.
3. Religious education means re-introducing students to Christ, his

message and his Church. In this way students are challenged to deepen their faith in Jesus and follow his way in their lives as members of his Church.

*The general aim*
The aim is to accompany the students in their life-story and to situate it within the overall Christian story. If we believe in Jesus and his message, then we believe that he has something to offer students in each and every aspect of their lives. Our role is to facilitate the encounter between students and the message of Jesus, to guide them as they discover the truth of this message in their lives. In this way we hope to give students a good grounding in the doctrines of the faith, as well as encouraging students to become faithful in their lives.

*The general method*
Each chapter in *Believe the Good News* follows the same basic process as the chapters in *A New Commandment*.

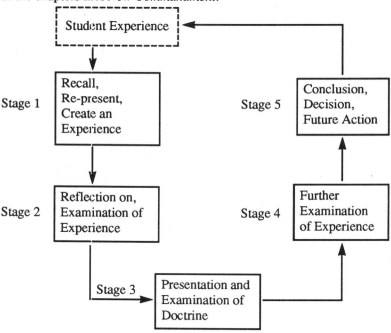

**Stage 1:** At the beginning of each chapter some 'starter' material is used to evoke a particular aspect of student experience. In some chapters the starter merely recalls or brings to mind an experience. For example, the questionnaire in Chapter 29 asks students to give their opinions on their experience of the Sacrament of Reconciliation. In other chapters the starter re-enacts or re-presents the experience in the classroom situation. For example, the story in Chapter 1 re-presents the

experience of growing up which all students have shared in some way. In a number of chapters the starter material is used to 'create' an experience for students in the classroom. For example, the Group Work exercise at the start of Chapter 35 is designed to give students an experience of disunity and lack of co-operation, so that they can better appreciate the value of unity and co-operation.

Often students will respond spontaneously to the starter, if given the opportunity to do so. The teacher should allow a few minutes for students to express their reactions, thoughts and feelings in relation to the starter, before going on to a systematic examination of it in Stage 2. This gives students an opportunity to enrich the learning experience by immediately linking the starter material with their own experience. For example, in response to the poem 'Mother and Daughter', Chapter 12, students usually give their own examples of parent/child relationships.

**Stage 2:** A number of questions are provided to enable students to examine in a more detailed way the experiences evoked by the starter material. In some cases the teacher may find that students have covered Stage 2 or most of it, in their spontaneous response to the starter. Other groups may have nothing much to say initially, and the questions provide them with a way into the experience.

Usually Stage 2 operates best on an oral level, but this should be adjusted to the needs of each group. A very noisy group, or a group lacking in confidence, may need to write down their ideas first and then call them out to the class. For academically weak students the teacher may wish to limit the number of questions and perhaps include more recall or comprehension questions before going ahead with simple analysis.

The effective use of Stages 1 and 2 are crucial to the success of the learning process. If Stage 1 is given sufficient attention, then the experience is made real for students, which is a primary factor in motivating learning in religious education. Stage 2, when it is covered well, enables students to discover something of the truth in and through their own experience. It gives them an opportunity to make judgments, and come to some conclusions as to the significance of the experience and its meaning.

**Stage 3:** Each chapter presents the Christian doctrine relevant to the experience evoked and explored in Stages 1 and 2. The doctrine is presented in one or more blocks of content. It usually summarises in 'official' language points raised in Stage 2. It also presents new material to students, designed to lead them to a richer understanding of the experience explored in Stages 1 and 2. The main doctrinal points made in each chapter are highlighted in coloured blocks.

We have not included questions or exercises on basic comprehension of the doctrinal content. Each teacher is best able to judge the level of questioning necessary to ensure that a particular class understands the basic text. With one class, the text may simply summarise what students have already expressed in their own words; then the teacher will only need to ask, 'What are the main points made in this paragraph?'; 'Are any new points made which we have not mentioned?' With another class, the teacher may need to ask questions such as, 'What does "irritable" mean?'; 'What is a Pastoral Letter?' etc.

**Stage 4:** One or more sets of exercises are provided which give students the opportunity to re-examine the experience explored in Stages 1 and 2 in light of what they have learned in Stage 3. The exercises are designed to help students look more deeply at their experience, and to challenge them with the Christian message relevant to that experience. For example, in Chapter 8 the experience of conscience is explored. The doctrine presents the Christian understanding of the informed conscience. The exercises challenge students to explore the value of an informed conscience, encourage them to evaluate how informed their consciences are and work out who informs their consciences.

Where a number of doctrinal points are raised by a particular starter, Stages 3 and 4 are repeated in the chapter.

**Stage 5:** At the end of each chapter, a number of opportunities are given to students to put into practice in some way in their lives what they have learned. Many of the assignments, projects and actions in the different chapters give students a chance to make a decision about how they will act, or think, or what attitudes they will adopt.

It is very important to give students an opportunity to complete Stage 5. It gives a satisfaction to them which reinforces what they have accomplished in Stages 1 to 4. Even if students decide not to allow what they have learned to change them, the very act of making a decision is an essential part of the learning process.

*The method is the message*

We have found that using these five stages helps students to learn both the doctrines of the faith and how to be faithful. But the method has another value which is equally important. It teaches students that the Christian message relates directly to them and to their experiences. It gives them a way of understanding the Christian message which they will be able to use even after they have left school.

This method is very respectful towards students, while at the same time presenting the Christian message in an uncompromising manner. It demands discipline and order from students while encouraging them to be creative and imaginative. The successful use of this method tends to facilitate a good relationship between religion teacher and students, which is essential for effective religious education.

Some teachers experience the 'doctrinal gap' problem when they are trying to relate to the needs of their students. Everything goes well for Stages 1 and 2; then, at Stage 3, the students 'switch off'. There are two likely reasons for this:

(a) The teacher does not give enough time for Stages 1 and 2 to be done in depth, with the result that students do not engage with the material on a personal level. This becomes obvious when the doctrine is presented. To counteract this problem it is essential to fully explore the experience in Stages 1 and 2, and to make sure that the students can identify with this experience in their own lives. For example, one teacher had difficulty teaching a deprived group of students about God's forgiveness. It emerged that none of the students had had a conscious experience of being forgiven, and so the doctrine made no sense to them. In order for Stage 3 to be effective, the experience evoked in Stages 1 and 2 must be real to the students. In some cases this may involve adapting the suggested starter material, or focusing on one small element within it in order to relate to the students' conscious experience. Even students who do not have a conscious experience of being forgiven experience the need for forgiveness, and the desire to be forgiven. This experience, if it is sensitively explored, can provide a very real basis for the appreciation of God's forgiveness.

(b) There can also be a problem if doctrine is presented as something 'to be learned, known, believed', rather than as offering a challenge, a help or a comfort. Doctrine should certainly be presented as Christian truth, with no apologies, but we must allow students to analyse it critically, 'try it on for size', and discover what truth the doctrine holds for them. Otherwise doctrine will appear to be a block of information instead of a real message of hope and love.

## PLANNING YOUR RELIGIOUS EDUCATION PROGRAMME

Until recently, it used to be sixth years who were critical, bored or even hostile in religion class. The phenomenon moved gradually down the school, until now even juniors are 'affected'. Today, many religion teachers consider 13 to 14-year-olds to be the hardest to teach. Many can be argumentative and hostile, while others may be apathetic and unresponsive. Because of their lack of knowledge and experience, many of their questions seem to require the old Irish answer, 'You can't get there from here!'

*Believe the Good News* is designed to help the religion teacher to motivate 13 to 14-year-old students, and to give students a good grounding in the basic knowledge necessary to understand both the Christian message and their own faith experience. If they have studied *A New Commandment*, they will have learned the basic concepts and knowledge upon which *Believe the Good News* is based. They will also be familiar with the method used, as outlined above.

*Knowing the students*
In order to choose the best resources and methods for each group of students, the teacher must make every effort to get to know students.

Obviously, if the teacher has taught a particular class the previous year, the task is a lot easier. Being involved with students outside class, in the local community or through extra-curricular activities in school, is always helpful. However, it is through classwork that the majority of teachers will come into contact most directly with students. The use of project work, group work, discussion, drama and other pupil-centred activities gives the teacher excellent opportunities to observe students without infringing on their privacy.

*Responding to the needs of students*
At this age, it is good to involve students to a limited extent in planning the religious education programme. At the beginning of the year students can be asked to submit a list of topics which they would like to study in religion class. The teacher can learn a lot about the class from the contents of such a list! Although you may get the occasional risqué topic thrown in to see how you react, general topics tend to underline how young and innocent these supposedly 'street-wise' youngsters are. With a less-able group, it can be useful to give a list of possible topics and allow students to choose from them.

Some 13 to 14-year-olds are captivated by excitement and mystery. Others are scornful of anything save the strictly factual. Decisions about topics, starters and content have to be made to take into account these and other variables. Naturally, the greatest difficulty arises when different views and opinions are represented strongly within one class group. In this situation, involving students in the decision-making process can be helpful. They can be encouraged to compromise, to accept that different people have different ideas, and to try to understand those who differ from them. This type of activity is an invaluable part of a religious education programme, since it involves putting Christian values into practice.

*Using the textbook*
*Believe the Good News* is divided into eight units. These are not intended to be taught consecutively. The first three units — Stewardship of God's Creation; Relationships; and Relationships in Trouble — are the core units. They introduce the basic experiences to be explored throughout the book. Units IV to VIII provide the Scriptural, Sacramental, Ecclesiastical, Liturgical and Spiritual context of those experiences. They are designed to help students explore the wider implications of their personal experience. It is hoped that, throughout the year, the teacher would choose from the units those resources which are best suited to a particular class at different stages. Obviously it would be helpful to study chapters from 'The Liturgical Year' at the appropriate times — Christmas, Lent, Easter and so on. Similarly, it would be helpful to gently introduce Prayer as a theme early in the year, and perhaps alternate oratory work with classwork right throughout the year.

*Themes*

It can be helpful with some students to use the textbook thematically. This is particularly so if the class is reasonably able intellectually, and sufficiently motivated to pursue a theme for a number of classes. (Less able students need more frequent changes of topic, and can return to study them in greater depth several times in the course of the year.)

Most chapters are relevant to more than one theme, but the following examples may indicate how a thematic approach could be implemented:

| | | |
|---|---|---|
| *Freedom* | Unit 1, | 'How Free Am I?', Chapter 6 |
| | Unit 2, | 'Adolescence', Chapter 10 |
| | Unit 4, | 'Exodus', Chapter 22 |
| *Sin and* | | |
| *Reconciliation* | Unit 1, | 'Free to Choose', Chapter 8 |
| | Unit 3, | 'Sin', Chapter 16 |
| | | 'The Breakdown of Relationships', Chapter 17 |
| | | 'Rebuilding Broken Relationships', Chapter 18 |
| | Unit 4, | 'Jesus' Death and Resurrection', Chapter 26 |
| | Unit 5, | 'Reconciliation', Chapter 29 |
| | Unit 7, | 'Lent', Chapter 38 |
| *Stewardship* | Unit 1, | 'My Response to God's Creation', Chapter 5 |
| | Unit 2, | 'Growing Up', Chapter 11 |
| | | 'Family', Chapter 12 |
| | | 'Friendship', Chapter 13 |
| | | 'Being a Steward to Myself', Chapter 15 |
| | Unit 4, | 'Jesus', Chapter 24 |
| | Unit 6, | 'The Church — Called to Serve', Chapter 32 |

## EDUCATION IN PERSONAL DEVELOPMENT

One of the most important themes in *Believe the Good News* is that of personal development of students. Many of the materials and exercises are designed to enable students to explore their own abilities and talents, to challenge their ideas about themselves, and to accompany them in their search for their true identity.

Education in personal development gives students a chance to become more aware of themselves as people, with physical, emotional, intellectual, social and spiritual needs. It enables them to value and respect themselves more highly, and to be more aware of their limitations without feeling crushed. Education in personal development gives students the opportunity to see the wholeness of their lives, in the context of God's love for them. Each teacher must make careful judgments in this area, so that any particular group of students will find that their specific needs and experiences are addressed in the classroom. No book or set of exercises, no matter how good, can replace the sensitive, caring and cheerful interest of the aware teacher.

*An approach to personal development*
*Believe the Good News* provides many resources to assist the teacher in this crucial area of education. The text situates personal development within the context of stewardship. 'As a human being, created and loved by God, and called to a loving relationship with God, I have many gifts and abilities, and a responsibility towards God, myself, others and the whole of creation.' *Believe the Good News* builds upon and develops the concepts and ideas introduced in *A New Commandment:* each person is special and unique, with talents and abilities; each one is faced with decisions and choices; our relationships with other people are an essential part of our lives; 'real happiness is possible only when I follow God's plan for my life and respond to God's loving invitation'. In *Believe the Good News*, these topics are explored in the context of growth, development and change, themes central to the experience of most 13 to 14-year-olds.

*The textbook as a resource*
Unit I of *Believe the Good News* explores the young adolescent's experience of uniqueness, giftedness, freedom, responsibility, power, conscience and responding to God in prayer and action.

Unit II focuses on the experience of early adolescence and puberty in the context of relationships with God, others and self. Unit III addresses the experience of failure and betrayal of relationships, and gives hope of reconciliation in a very practical way. It also provides an opportunity for students to look at the area of death and suffering, of which they are beginning to become aware as young adolescents.

Units IV to VIII provide the Scriptural, Sacramental, Ecclesiastical, Liturgical and Spiritual context of these experiences. They are designed to help students explore the wider implications of their personal experience and development.

It is intended that the teacher would choose from the units, or indeed from individual chapters, those particular stories, exercises and blocks of content which are best suited to the needs of one specific group of students.

For example, suppose there is a class of average intellectual ability, very vocal and demanding, quite self-centred as individuals in a rather thoughtless way, and tending towards disunity because a number of cliques have evolved in the class. This is a typical scenario for a group which has been together for a year or so and is confident of its position in the school. The teacher may feel that the group needs to look more closely at its relationships, both as a class and in the wider world of home and community. The group may need to discover ways in which it can affect other people by the way it treats them, and to explore the possibility of putting the Christian faith into practice in the context of relationships.

*Personal development - improving my relationships*
To facilitate the students' personal development in this area, the teacher might choose from the following resources in the textbook:
(a) 'My Response to God's Creation', Chapter 5. The teacher could encourage students to pay special attention to their stewardship of other people, and lay great emphasis on exercises 2 and 3, 'How can you act as a steward of creation at home?' and 'How can you act as a steward of creation at school?'. The teacher could go on to the topic of stewardship of each other as a class, why it is important and what problems arise when students do not act as stewards towards each other.

A very important point here is that the teacher is not trying to tell students how to treat each other. If there is to be real learning, i.e. a change in behaviour, then students must work out the answers for themselves. The teacher's role is in guidance, motivation and facilitation.

Students may come up with a suitable Action as an alternative to the one suggested in the chapter. For example, they might try listening to each other's opinions in religion class, and really trying to understand what others think. Or they might agree to treat each other politely (no pushing, shoving or worse!) for one day, as an expression of stewardship. From the teacher's side, the emphasis should not be on 'Being nice and good' but rather on 'Would you really be capable of this difficult task?'. Students will often respond to a challenge, when they will reject an appeal to their better natures! An evaluation of the success of the Action can be done afterwards. The emphasis here should be 'who really tried to do the action?; 'Why did it work/not work?'; Would it be worth doing again?'. An unsuccessful action is as useful as a successful one. Being a steward is very difficult, though not impossible. Getting rid of bad habits is also difficult. It is much easier to be a steward if everyone else is trying to be one also.

The purpose of this chapter, from the point of view of personal development, is not to make students into paragons of virtue overnight, but rather to open up the idea in their minds, to start them thinking.

(b) The teacher might go on to 'How Free Am I', Chapter 6. This chapter focuses on the early adolescent's experience of freedom and limitation. It also places great emphasis on 'how I use my freedom'. In the context of personal development in relationships, the teacher might encourage students to explore more deeply how they can use their freedom to help or hinder others. Questions 5 and 6 (page 26) refer to situations in the game, in which a student deliberately helped other people. The first set of exercises on this page can be used to explore 'how I use my freedom in my relationships at home, at school etc.', with a little guidance from the teacher. The last exercise on the page, 'What do you do that limits the freedom of other people?', can be applied directly to the classroom situation. The purpose here is to give students an opportunity to see themselves as *actors*, rather than passive *reactors* in their relationships. Many 13 to 14-year-olds are ready, if encouraged, to go beyond the instinctive 'I *had* to hit him, sir, because he stole my book/laughed at me' or whatever.

(c) In 'Free to Choose', Chapter 8, students are given an opportunity to discover the meaning of conscience. The teacher can guide them towards an exploration of the role of conscience in personal relationships by encouraging students to consider the effects of Ellen's and Peter's action on their relationships with their parents. Exercise 4 (page 35) and exercises 1 and 2 (page 37) also provide opportunities to examine the role of conscience in personal relationships. This is often a novel idea to students. For example, they tend to see obedience or disobedience to parents as the key issue, rather than the effect which obedience might have on their relationship with their parents. Usually they can quote many examples from their own experience once they have seen the connection. This has the added value of raising the consideration of conscience from what might become a purely legalistic approach to the topic, to a relational approach more in keeping with the basic Christian message of love.

(d) At this point, the teacher might consider students ready to study the units on relationships and the breakdown of relationships. The most important chapters from the point of view of personal development in relationships would be 'Adolescence', Chapter 10; 'Family', Chapter 12; 'Friendship', Chapter 13; 'God's Call and My Response', Chapter 14; 'Sin', Chapter 16; 'The Breakdown of Relationships', Chapter 17; and 'Rebuilding Broken Relationships', Chapter 18.

(e) The teacher might choose 'Jesus', Chapter 24 to help students understand more clearly how Jesus asks us to relate to one another and treat each other. The chapter focuses on the use and abuse of power. This is linked to the concept of stewardship, and the teacher might encourage students to examine the power which they have and use in their relationships. The questions (page 136) and exercise 2(d) and (e) (page 137) would be particularly useful here. The action is also very appropriate, although the class could come up with its own alternative. It is important for the teacher to bring the focus back again and again to relationships within the class — without, of course, being intrusive or 'psychoanalysing' students. Rather, the teacher's questions can encourage students to focus on an area which they might otherwise neglect.

(f) From the unit on Sacraments, the teacher might choose 'The Presence of Jesus', Chapter 28, and emphasise the aspect of being present to each other as class members (exercise 5, page 153 and exercise 2, page 154). It might also be helpful to explore how the risen Jesus is present with us in the classroom (exercises 1 and 4, page 155).

'Reconciliation', Chapter 29 and 'The Eucharist', Chapter 30 focus on the sacramental celebration of repentance and forgiveness, of sacrifice, thanksgiving and self-giving, all of which are a necessary part of our relationships. The teacher might consider it appropriate to facilitate the class in organising a penitential service and a Eucharistic celebration when the appropriate chapters have been studied. The emphasis in these celebrations should be on classroom relationships, on at least one occasion in the year. An advantage here is that students see the direct link between a classroom exploration of their attitudes towards and experience of relationships, and the sacramental celebrations.

(g) The unit on the Liturgical Year gives the teacher an opportunity to widen students' horizons and helps them to discover, that through the Church's year, they are given the opportunity to improve their relationships. Each of these chapters, from Advent to Pentecost, has its relationship aspect, which the teacher may choose to emphasise. For example, 'Advent', Chapter 36, exercises 1 and 2 (page 205) can be applied to our relationships; 'Christmas', Chapter 37, exercises 1 and 2 (page 207); 'Lent', Chapter 38, exercise 2 (page 213), exercise 1 (page 214) and exercises 1 and 2 (page 215); 'Easter', Chapter 39, exercises 1 and 2 (page 225); 'Pentecost', Chapter 40, exercises 1, 2 and 3 (page 231). In most of these chapters the action is also appropriate for personal development in relationships.

(h) The teacher might choose to use the example of Mary, as outlined in Chapter 41, as a model of how to relate to others. The exercises on page 235 can be used to emphasise Mary's love and commitment in her relationships, and students can examine their own relationships to see how following Mary's example might improve them.

(i) The teacher might choose 'Prayer', Chapter 42 to enable students to explore the place and value of prayer in their relationships. Prayer is presented as sharing our lives with God, and one of the most important aspects of our lives is our relationships. The starting exercise in Chapter 42 will help students evaluate the link between prayer and relationships in their lives. Exercise 2 (page 239) 'How can we worship God' in each of the following situations, (a) at school, (b) at home, (c) with friends, is a further opportunity to explore the place of relationships in our spiritual life. The action at the end of this chapter encourages students to build up their relationships with God and each other through the formation of a prayer group.

(j) From Unit VI, 'The Christian Community', the teacher might choose 'The Church — called to serve', Chapter 32, to help students explore their relationships in the context of the parish community. The two sets of exercises (page 183) are helpful in this regard, as is exercise 2 (page 185). The discussion and reflection at the end of this chapter are also useful, emphasising the giving and serving aspect of relationships.

*Meeting the needs of students*
A similar analysis of the resources in the textbook will produce materials and exercises suitable for a detailed study of many other aspects of personal development, for example, spiritual development, moral development, the development of self-esteem and self-confidence etc. The aim should be to identify the most important needs and experiences of students in a particular class, to use the textbook (with other resources if desired) to respond to those needs, and facilitate exploration of these experiences.

Based on the initial response of the class, the teacher must decide carefully what to choose or emphasise from material available. If a class is particularly young and immature, then the depth of analysis and application achieved will be less than if the class is highly motivated, very able and with a strong faith background.

A highly motivated class would be able to spend some weeks studying exclusively the theme of personal development. Most 13 to 14-year-olds would not be able for such an intensive course, and for them it might be best to focus at intervals on personal development in the context of another topic. For example, when teaching the topic of Christmas, the teacher might devote one class, or a part of one class, to the question of 'preparing for Christmas by improving my relationships at home, at school and with my friends'.

*Sex education*
Sexual development is an important element in personal development. Sexual development is concerned with the overall development of the person as a male or female human being. In many schools the religion teacher is expected to include sex education in the religious education programme. However, sex education is an inter-disciplinary subject and, where possible, it should be planned and implemented by a number of teachers in different subject areas. The ethos of the school and wishes of parents must inform any such programme of sex education.

With such a programme in operation, the role of the religion teacher could be to help students explore their experience of sexuality in the context of their physical, social, emotional, moral and spiritual development. In this context, the religion teacher would be building on the students' prior knowledge of their physical development and their awareness of emotional and social change.

*Believe the Good News* approaches the student's sexual development from this view-point. It does not aim to give a comprehensive account of the physical changes which occur in puberty, for example. That is not the function of a religion textbook. However, if no comprehensive programme of sex education is operating within the school, the religion teacher (with the support of the school management and parents) may wish to include a comprehensive account of the physical and emotional changes and developments which occur in puberty and early adolescence, as part of the religious education programme.

There are many books and programmes available to help you in the task, and it could be worthwhile to invest in a set of books for the school.

However, you may find it useful to prepare your own handouts, overheads and diagrams, which you can then adapt specifically to the needs of any particular group. We include here a suggested handout suitable for a group of average ability, who are not clear on basic human physiology or appropriate sexual terminology.

*The development of female reproductive organs*
In adolescence a girl becomes physically able to become a mother. Her sex glands, or ovaries, start to produce an ovum about once a month. This is called *ovulation*.

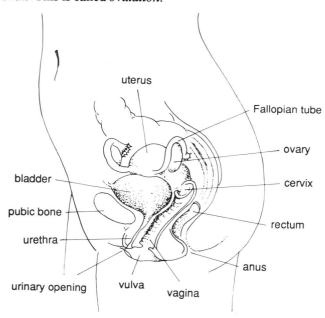

*The Female Reproductive Organs*

After sexual intercourse, the ovum can join with one sperm and form a new human being. A special lining grows inside the girl's womb. This will help a new human being to grow and develop. When the girl does not become pregnant, the ovum dies. Later in the month, the lining of the womb comes away and leaves the girl's body through her vagina. This is called *menstruation*. The girl's breasts start to develop so that when she has a baby she will be able to feed him or her.

*The development of male reproductive organs*
In adolescence, a boy becomes physically able to be a father. His penis and scrotum get larger, and his testicles start to produce sperm. During sexual intercourse, the sperm travel through the erect penis into the woman's vagina. This is called *ejaculation.* If the woman is ovulating, one sperm can join with the ovum and form a new human being. The other sperm die.

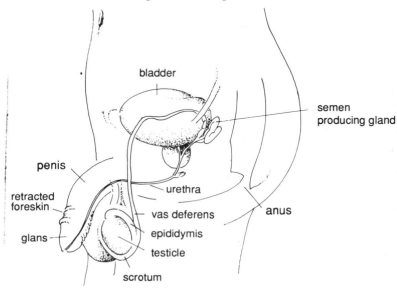

*The Male Reproductive and Urinary Systems*

When sexual intercourse does not take place, the sperm can be absorbed back into the boy's body and disposed of by the excretory system. Sometimes an ejaculation takes place when the boy is asleep. This is called a *nocturnal emission,* or 'wet dream'.

Comprehensive sex education is a specialist discipline, and we strongly advise religion teachers who intend to include it as part of their religious education programme to become qualified in this area by attending any suitable courses available.
You may also find the following books useful: *Ready, Steady, Grow, preparing young people for life* by Angela McNamara, Veritas Publications 1986; *A Teacher's Guide to Resource Material on Relationships/Sex Education* edited by Donal O'Mahony, Veritas Publications 1987.
As with any other subject, it is vital that the teacher should feel comfortable and knowledgeable in the area of sexuality. It is very difficult to remain sensitive to the needs and fears of students if we ourselves are feeling inadequate or embarrassed. If the religion teacher

feels uncomfortable about teaching sex education, and no other teacher in the school is willing to take on the task, then it may be appropriate to bring in a speaker, or team, to teach sex education. Normally the speaker(s) will meet both parents and students (in separate groups). Some branches of the Catholic Marriage Advisory Council are able to provide teams to do this work. In this situation, it is vital for the teacher to meet with the speaker(s) well in advance to plan the programme and make sure that it is appropriate to the needs of students.

*Sexual relationships*
Some 13 to 14-year-olds (though by no means all) are interested in or have experience of 'going out' with members of the opposite sex. If it should arise that the topic of 'boyfriends and girlfriends' is of interest to a particular group of students, then it would be useful to include a lesson or two on this topic as part of the religious education programme. It is very important, however, to make clear to the class that it is perfectly normal and quite common for people to be 16, 17 or even older before having a boyfriend or girlfriend.

'Friendship', Chapter 13, would be a good basis from which to develop a lesson on sexual relationships. A good starting exercise is to divide the class into groups of five or six students. If your school is co-educational, put boys and girls into separate groups.
Task No.1: What do boys expect from girls?
Task No.2: What do girls expect from boys?
Give the groups a maximum of ten minutes to decide on their answers. As each group gives its report, record the points briefly on the chalkboard or flipchart, in two separate columns, one for each task. Underline or highlight in some way answers given by more than one group. A number of exercises can then follow:
   (a) In a co-educational school — were the girls' answers different to those given by the boys? Why/why not?
   (b) In a single-sex school — what answers do you think members of the opposite sex would have given to these questions? (If there are any new points made here, add them to the lists.)
   (c) Let the class summarise the main points made in each list.
   (d) From the evidence in the lists, do boys and girls expect to be friends with one another? Do they expect honesty, loyalty, consideration, fun, etc. from each other? Why/why not?
   (e) How could boys and girls improve their relationships with each other?

In some classes, the issue of 'going steady' may arise, although the vast majority of 13 to 14-year-olds will not have had even the token 3-week-long relationship. Again, the emphasis should be on students' understanding and experience of what 'going steady' means. We should be wary of going beyond the students' actual experience. Naturally, much of their 'information' will come from teenage magazines and television programmes. It is useful at times to come back to such questions as, 'Is that what happens in *this* school/town/community?' or

'What do you think should happen in such a situation?'.

Once students have explored their experience and ideas on the subject, the teacher should present the basic Christian message relevant to the level reached by students in their exploration. For example, the basic message relevant to friendship (Chapter 13) can be reiterated in the context of boy/girl relationships. The basic message about the true meaning of love can be given in the context of more serious relationships e.g. 1 Cor. 12:4-8. Students can then apply this message to their experience and see if it could help improve their relationships. The teacher should present the Christian message in a positive way, as a way of helping relationships, rather than as a set of 'do's' and 'don't's'.

## TEACHING THROUGH DRAMA

It has long been recognised that use of drama in the classroom can have numerous benefits. Drama can be used to explore new experiences or to gain deeper understanding of present experience. Students who might otherwise remain silent in class can very often be more easily motivated to contribute by acting than by speaking or writing. Self-expression through the use of drama can help to improve relationships within the class, increase levels of tolerance and co-operation, and foster confidence and self-assurance. A further advantage is that students tend to remember very vividly what they learn through the stimulating medium of drama.

*Preparation and planning*

The successful use of drama in the classroom is the result of careful preparation and planning. The teacher needs to be clear about the type of activity to be attempted and in what way it is to be of benefit to students. The same material will not necessarily be useful with different classes, even in the same year-group. Careful consideration must be given to the needs of the group in question — their maturity, interest and ability.

Students must be *taught* how to learn through drama. From the beginning the teacher must lay down certain rules which are *always* followed when the class does drama. The nature of these rules will vary from group to group, and, generally, the fewer and simpler they are, the better for everyone. For example, everyone must pay full attention when another student or group is presenting their work; no shouting or horseplay of any kind is allowed.

When organising a class based on drama, the teacher should follow these (or similar) guidelines:

1. A specific task should be set for each student or group. (Written instructions can be helpful.)
2. If students are working in groups, then all the rules for group-work apply, including the appointment of a leader or director for the group.
3. Each student or group must be given the opportunity to 'perform'.

This means in practice that more than one class period will be required if individual performances are more than two or three minutes long.
4. It is essential to allow time for comments on and evaluation of the performances. The important point to be addressed is not, 'Were they any good?' but rather, 'What message does this performance have for us?'.

Occasionally, the teacher may wish to start class with a short piece of drama, performed by only one or two members of the class, before going on to explore further material which is not dramatic in form. This can be a useful technique, provided it is not always the same few people who are allowed to perform. However no student should be forced to take part in drama, though we may strongly encourage them to do so. Other tasks can always be found for the genuinely unable; 'stage' and 'props' manager; prompter; organiser; 'judge' (leading the evaluations at the end); journalist/reviewer of the performances etc. Students with a serious learning or social disability can be 'advertisers', designing or even simply colouring in posters 'announcing' performances.

*Dramatic activities suitable for the classroom*
**Improvisation:** Students are given a brief outline of a scene and the characters involved. They are not given a script or the outcome of the scene. This requires spontaneity and openness on the part of students, who are given very little time to prepare, and who must 'invent' the situation as they go along. Examples:
  (a) Two boys are walking down a street discussing the foul which the referee missed in yesterday's football match;
  (b) Some girls are talking about a new girl in the class whom they do not like. The new girl joins them. What happens?

**Role-play:** Students are given specific characters in some detail, and told that they are in a specific situation. How do they react? They are not given a script, or the outcome of the situation. The students must be given some time in which to 'get into' the roles they have been given. Example: A family situation, with a detailed character for each member. Mother, harried and anxious, certain that her daughter is mitching from school. Father, very involved in his work and other voluntary activities in the parish, spends very little time at home. He thinks it's the mother's place to 'mind' the daughter. The daughter is 14, hates school and mitches whenever she can, because she is bullied by other students. She is afraid to get into trouble at home but she is also terrified of the bullies. The mother decides to confront the daughter at dinner on Friday night, when the father is present.

**Plays:** Students are given or are asked to compose a script for certain characters in a particular situation. Students need time to plan, write and rehearse the play. Example: (a) Saturday night at the disco; (b) Christmas morning.

**Mime:** Students are given details about a situation which they must portray without the use of words. The emphasis here is on movement, gesture and use of facial expression to convey meaning. This is a particularly useful way to allow students to express everyday feelings and to explore them. Examples: (a) You wake up in the pitch dark in a small cave, with one tiny opening, barely big enough for you to squeeze out. Outside you find yourself in a tunnel...; (b) You have had a row with your friend, and you have to sit beside him/her in class all day.

*Suggested uses for drama in religious education*
Drama can be used with many topics in religious education. It can be used in the classroom, as part of an ordinary lesson, or in the oratory as one element in a liturgy or prayer-service. Examples: as part of a reconciliation service, students might dramatise the story of the Prodigal Son, or any other experience of sin/forgiveness/reconciliation they have had.

In the classroom, students might act out different versions of the story of the Prodigal Son. Each group would require six or seven actors, i.e. father, two sons, one or two friends of the younger son, one or two servants of the household.

Group 1: the story of the Prodigal Son as it is given in Scripture.
Group 2: the story of the Prodigal Son changed so that the father rejects the son when he returns.
Group 3: the story changed so that the father welcomes the son back under strict conditions as to his future conduct.
Group 4: the story changed so that the younger son does not find the courage to come home.

The purpose of this exercise is to highlight the true meaning of the story told by Jesus, which we sometimes take for granted. The plays/role-plays should highlight for students the nature and consequences of sin, the joy and happiness of forgiveness and reconciliation, and the great love of God as shown in Jesus' story.

Some suggestions are given in the textbook for the use of drama, but the teacher could include many more dramatic exercises and activities. For example, when an exercise asks for examples, or requires students to write a story, the teacher can allow students to do this work through drama: instead of giving examples of situations in which young people have to use their conscience, students can do role-plays of these situations (Chapter 8).

As with any other procedure in the classroom, over-use will diminish the value of drama. It should be a privilege and a treat for students to learn through drama. When students show that they are willing to work hard, co-operate with each other and obey the rules, then drama can be used as a regular classroom activity.

## GUIDE TO TERMS: PUPIL TEXT

*Questions:* Intended to be answered orally by the students.
*Exercises:* Intended mainly to be used as short written work. Some may involve simple research.
*Assignments:* These generally involve some research by the students with a written report.

*Projects:* The term project is used to describe a multi-media presentation of a topic studied in some depth by students. A project can be undertaken individually or in groups. A class project can be undertaken if each student (or small group) takes one or more aspects of the same topic. The class project might be 'Creation'. The class can be divided into groups. Each group might take a different aspect of creation and find out as much information as possible about it. This information should then be presented using drawing, painting, collage, photographs, graphs, diagrams, maps, written work, models, drama etc. Project work has many benefits. Students acquire knowledge both as a result of their own study and by learning from each other's presentations. (The more interesting and varied the presentations, the more will be learned.) Students develop confidence and pride in themselves both as individuals and as a group. If the teacher encourages students to 'stretch' themselves and welcomes new ideas, less able students in particular can benefit enormously. However, the less able do need very close supervision and a lot of teacher input, ideas and encouragement. A good rule for the less able is that they should present the same information in as many different ways as possible.

*Group work:* This is intended to be used for both oral and written work. Group work must be very specific and controlled to be useful as a learning exercise. Thirteen to fourteen-year-old students must be given practical work to do in groups — writing, drawing, creating plays.

*How to do group work*
1. Give all instructions before the groups are formed.
2. Make sure each student has the necessary materials (paper, pens, colours etc.).
3. Give specific questions to which written answers are required. Give each group a copy of the questions. If every group is to answer the same questions, these can be put on the board or flipchart.
4. Set a time limit — and stick to it.
5. If necessary, ask each student to do individual work first before going into groups to share results. (This is to ensure that the work is not left to, or appropriated by, the diligent or dominant few.)
6. Groups can be organised as follows: give each student a number (depending on the number of groups required). For example, if you need six groups, number the students from one to six. All students with the same number form one group. Explain in advance exactly where the number ones will work, the number twos and so on.
7. Appoint a secretary/reporter in each group.
8. When the time limit is up, disband the groups. Each students goes back to his/her place. (Otherwise there is the temptation for the groups to keep on working and distract the class during the presentation of reports.)
9. Allow each secretary to report on his/her group's work. If the

work is a project, it can be displayed in a suitable manner.
10. When all the groups have given their reports, the teacher can summarise the findings.

**Discussion:** This teaching technique is introduced in *Believe the Good News* primarily as a foundation for learning through discussion at senior level. We hope that the teacher will take the opportunity to teach students *how* to discuss, and allow them to practise discussion occasionally throughout the year. It is not intended to be a primary teaching technique at this level. However, it can be quite difficult to teach 15 to 16-year-olds about discussion, so it is worthwhile to introduce it early, before students acquire too many bad habits!

The purpose of discussion is to enable students to explore and evaluate critically their ideas, attitudes and opinions. Discussion is not a format suitable for giving new information to students. However, through discussion students may alter or adapt their attitudes in light of teacher questioning or the input of other students.

Whether the topic chosen for discussion is one suggested by textbook or by students, the following guidelines should be followed.

*Preparation*
1. The topic for discussion should be a popular one for the majority of the students — otherwise the teacher will end up giving a monologue!
2. The topic should be decided well in advance — at least the day before — to give students a chance to think about it.
3. The topic should be helpfully phrased; for example, 'Heavy metal music makes young people violent' is a better topic than 'Heavy metal'.
4. If possible, arrange the classroom furniture in such a way that each student can see everyone in the class in comfort. Where this is impossible, it may be necessary to relax the rules regarding students turning around in their seats.

*Discussion*
1. Explain clearly to students what is expected of them during the discussion. (This will not be necessary after a time.)
2. Introduce the topic briefly, and ask basic recall and comprehension questions to make clear what exactly it is we intend to discuss, e.g. What is heavy metal music? Why do some people think it is violent? How do heavy metal bands behave on stage, etc.? This is an essential part of a discussion — just what exactly are we talking about? If too many issues emerge at this stage, the teacher could invite the class to choose which aspect of the topic they will address that day. It is more helpful to have several short (one-class period) discussions, than a long, rambling discussion that limps from one class period to the next.
3. Ask students for their opinions about the topic. Encourage them to comment on each other's views. Some students have a

tendency to talk only to the teacher and ignore the rest of the class. The danger here is of confrontation between teacher and student over a matter of opinion. It is helpful for the teacher to listen to the students' points of view and, rather than giving his/her own opinion, ask, 'What do the rest of you think about that? Do you agree/disagree? Why/why not?'.

The exception here is if a student makes an incorrect statement, e.g. 'If you are 14, you can get a driving licence.' The teacher should correct any factual errors, but must remember that opinions are neither right or wrong. You may certainly encourage students to justify their attitudes and opinions with factual evidence. It is generally better if the teacher gives no personal opinions unless asked, and, even then, these should be given at the end of the discussion.

4. The teacher should encourage students to come to some agreement about the topic under discussion. In particular, an effort should be made to balance the more extreme views in the class.
5. Each member of the class should be given the opportunity to come to a conclusion about the topic they have just discussed. Have they learned anything new? Will the discussion influence their future thought/action?

It is very important to end a discussion rather than leave it in mid-air. This requires firm time-keeping by the teacher. It also means ensuring that the topic chosen is not too broad to be dealt with adequately in the time available. Students may be asked to write a brief report on the discussion and, as time goes on, to evaluate their discussion skills.

*Reflection:* This is a short passage from Scripture relating to some aspect of the topic covered in a particular chapter. It is suggested that, in a classroom setting, the reflection be used in conjunction with the prayer, as follows:
1. Students and teacher adopt a prayerful attitude in silence — sitting, standing, or kneeling.
2. A quiet, meditative atmosphere is created through the use of quiet music, a short breathing exercise or a short relaxation exercise (e.g. becoming aware of your breathing, counting your breaths in and out, relaxing each part of your body from head to toe etc.).
3. The teacher (or a student) reminds the group of the presence of God among them, and especially His presence in His word.
4. One person reads the reflection slowly and carefully while everyone else listens with eyes closed.
*or*
One person reads the reflection and the others follow the passage in their religion book.
*or*
Everyone reads the passage quietly aloud (only if it is short).
*or*
Everyone reads the passage silently.

5. A few minutes are given to thinking silently about the passage. The teacher may help by giving one or two short comments on the passage.
6. Everyone prays the prayer together.
7. It is good to end with the Sign of the Cross.

*Action:*
(a) Some actions are designed to be undertaken privately by students. The teacher can give a few minutes to students to reflect upon the action. (This might take place during the reflection/prayer experience.)
(b) Other actions are designed for classroom use. The teacher must decide how much time (if any) to give to this type of action.

*Song:* Songs have been chosen which are appropriate to the theme of each chapter. Sometimes one or more verses are particularly apt. Even if a particular song is not taught to students, relevant verses could be used as alternative reflections.

## GUIDE TO TERMS: TEACHER'S BOOK

*The aim:* This is what the teacher hopes to do in the lesson. (It may take more than one class period.)

*The objective:* This is what the pupils will achieve or be able to do as a result of the lesson.

*Number of class periods required:* This is the minimum number of forty-minute class periods required to achieve the aims and objectives. It does not include time needed for the researching, writing or presentation of projects or assignments, or the carrying out of class-based actions.

*Starters/alternative starters:* This refers to the experiential exercises with which the topics are introduced.

*Related themes:* This refers to the themes which are developed explicitly or implicitly in the chapter. Most of these themes are based on the concepts and doctrines introduced in *A New Commandment.*

# PART II  CLASSWORK

You may wish to take one or more introductory classes before using the textbook itself. We have found the following activities useful for this kind of class.

1. If you have not taught this group of students previously, and you do not know them very well, then you could devote part of a class to the anonymous filling in of simple 'curriculum vitae'. The teacher collects these at the end of class, collates the material and on the following day presents the findings to the class.

    *Sample questionnaire or curriculum vitae:*
    Age:
    Sex:
    Favourite school subject:
    Favourite T.V. programme:
    Favourite sport:
    Favourite food:
    Favourite colour:
    Hobbies:
    Likes:
    Dislikes:
    Fears:
    Ambitions:
    Dreams:
    Worst disappointment:
    Best achievement:
    What I expect from religion class this year:
    What I enjoyed about religion class last year:
    What I disliked about religion class last year:

2. Each member of the class can prepare a 'personality poster'. For this they will need colour pens or pencils, old magazines, scissors, glue and a large sheet of poster paper. (If necessary, they can use the middle page of their religion copy.) They are to represent their 'personality' on the page — their likes, dislikes, talents, feelings, opinions. If possible, no words should be used. Black can be used to denote 'dislike', red can denote liking, and so on. When the posters are finished, they can be displayed in the classroom. As a further exercise, each student can present his/her poster to the class and explain what it means.

3. With a class you know well, the teacher can encourage students to talk about their experiences during holidays, how they feel about coming back to school, what they expect from (a) school, (b) the religion class this year. If the class is inclined to be noisy or undisciplined, they can write down their views and then call them out during the class.

4. If the class know each other well, and you don't know them, then they can 'introduce' themselves to you (a) in pairs, each one

introducing the other, (b) as a class — what they are like as a class, good points, bad points, likes, dislikes etc.
5. It is useful to explain to students that while you have prepared a religious education programme for them for the year, you would welcome their suggestions and ideas. These can be recorded on the flipchart or chalkboard and then voted on by the class. As a rule it is wise to get a two-thirds majority in favour of a topic before accepting it. If any topics are patently unsuitable, e.g. 'Videos' or 'Open-heart surgery', the teacher should explain why. The teacher must have absolute right of veto on any topic or activity. However, many apparently unfruitful topics can be incorporated successfully into the course to the great satisfaction of all concerned, e.g. 'Football hooliganism' can be looked at in the context of conscience, sin, relationships and responsibility; 'Heavy metal and its effects on young people' can be discussed in the context of adolescence, conscience and making decisions. If you are unsure of the suitability of a topic, put a question-mark after it and tell the class you will have to think about that one. Be sure to get back to them with your decision.
6. Another useful exercise to give students early in the term is a mini-examination in what they were supposed to have learned the previous year, or what they are presumed to know. It can be very instructive for both teacher and students to discover exactly how much students do or do not know. Many students who claim to 'know all about that' are quite taken aback to find that there are some areas in which they could improve. With a less able group, a suitably set 'exam' can do wonders for their self-esteem as they realise that they know far more than they thought.

The 'exam' can be given in traditional question and answer written form, or it could be given as a multiple choice paper. Better still, the teacher could divide the class into teams and conduct a knock-out quiz. (Be sure to organise the groups as fairly as possible so that all the more-able students don't end up in one group.)

## UNIT I: STEWARDSHIP OF GOD'S CREATION
## CHAPTER 1: ME

*Aims of Lesson 1*
1. To present the idea of a person's life as a story.
2. To show that other people have an influence on the life of an individual.
3. To remind students that each person is unique and special, and loved by God.

*Objectives of Lesson 1*
1. That students will describe their life stories.
2. That they will identify the people who have had the most influence on their lives.

3.  That they will explore (briefly) their experiences of feeling good about themselves or feeling bad about themselves.

*Number of class periods required* 2

*Development of lesson*
1. Starter, questions, first body of content, first set of exercises.
2. Group work to the end of the chapter.

***Starter:*** The starter in this chapter focuses on the experience of growing up, with all the changes involved in that process. Jim's problem is one of self-esteem or self-confidence, which took a blow when he was no longer brilliant at basketball. Many students will experience low self-esteem and other negative feelings also. Unlike Jim, their stories may not have reached a happy ending, so it is essential to be sensitive here. When the students are examining Jim's story, it would be appropriate to ask them, 'Is this a typical life-story? Are there many people like Jim?' Remember, they do not have to like Jim or believe in him for the starter to be effective. If they come up with their own more 'realistic' stories, so much the better. Even students who come from the most supportive of homes will experience problems at times and it is good to recognise this in the religion class. Just because you are having problems, it does not mean that you are a bad or unusual person, or that you come from a 'bad' home.

***Discussion:*** Many students, especially boys, are judged by their peers on the basis of how involved or interested they are in sport. If this is an issue in your school, then it would be useful to have the first discussion at some stage in the first term. While it is doubtful that one discussion will radically change the students' outlook (which many of them have picked up from adults, in any case), it can give them something to think about, and can be reassuring for the 'non-sporty' types.

The second discussion can be addressed from a number of different angles: Do you always do what your friends want? Would you prefer if your parents or your friends trusted you, liked your clothes, praised you? In what ways do your friends influence you? Your parents? Others? Do they all have equal influence?

***Action:*** If the class has not been together as a group for very long, it may be best to use this action later in the term when they have got to know one another better.

***Related themes:*** The uniqueness of each person; God's love and care; family; adolescence; personal development.

# CHAPTER 2: STORY

*Aims of Lesson 2*
1. To explain the power that stories can have and how they can affect people.
2. To show that stories which tell us about our faith, and especially Scripture stories, have many true messages and meanings which can affect our lives.

*Objectives of Lesson 2*
1. That students will explore what stories mean, and have meant to them, and how they have been affected by stories.
2. That they will identify the message or meaning in a familiar Scripture story.

*Number of class periods required* 2

*Development of lesson*
1. Starter, questions, first body of content, and exercise 1.
2. Exercise 2 to the end of the chapter.

**Starter:** The theme of story and the effect which stories have on our lives is one of the most important in *Believe the Good News*.

**Story:** It is important for the teacher to identify in advance the kind of story which appeals to students. They may not associate the word 'story' with their favourite Australian soap opera; they may not realise that a film, a cartoon strip and an advertisement can all be stories. Many students will never have thought about the effects which different stories have on their lives. At this stage, the teacher must be wary of pushing students beyond their capacity for self-analysis. It is good to help the students to identify the kind of 'story' they enjoy. Then the teacher can encourage them to think back to the stories they liked as young children. Many parents tell their children 'warning' stories, to keep them out of danger, and some students will remember these. Perhaps a story influenced the games they played — pirates because of *Treasure Island,* cowboys and Indians because of a John Wayne film. Students can then be encouraged to come to conclusions about the effects of stories on 'some people', even if they cannot accept that they are now influenced by stories.

Students of this age are very eager to maintain their dignity, and may feel threatened by the idea that they are not at all times in control of their responses. The idea of a story 'doing' things to them may not be at all acceptable to some students! Such students are often happier to identify the message or meaning in a story, since this preserves their right to accept or reject the message consciously.

**Action:** For less able students, explain briefly that a Christian message is one in which people are encouraged to be loving towards one another, and respect each other as human beings. With a more-able group, encourage them to work out what would be involved in a 'Christian message', and encourage them to re-evaluate their definition when they present their examples.

***Related themes:*** Learning from Scripture; the parables of Jesus; the Creation story; the history of salvation; the Exodus story; the story of Adam and Eve; the Prodigal Son; the Infancy narratives; the story of the first Pentecost.

## CHAPTER 3: MY WORLD

*Aims of Lesson 3*
1. To give students some information on scientific theories of the origin of the universe.
2. To give them some information on scientific theories of the origin of life.
3. To explain the Christian belief about Creation.
4. To give students an opportunity to appreciate the beauty, wonder and greatness of Creation.

*Objectives of Lesson 3*
1. That students will describe their experience of being alive on a small planet in a vast universe.
2. That they will be able to describe in their own words why life is possible on earth, and that they will have a greater awareness of the multiplicity of life-forms on the planet.
3. That they will explore the Genesis account of Creation, explain its message or meaning, and show in what ways it differs in purpose from scientific accounts of the origins of the universe.
4. That they will explore the extracts from Psalms 19 and 65, and note the thoughts and feelings which correspond to their own response to creation.

*Number of class periods required* 2

*Development of lesson*
1. Starter, first body of content, exercises, second body of content and exercise 1.
2. Exercise 2 to the end of the chapter.

***Project/alternative starter:*** The number of class periods required does not include project work. We would strongly recommend that students do the project on 'Creation' suggested at the end of the chapter. Indeed, for many groups this would be an excellent alternative starter. Some students of this age have a great interest in space, pre-historic 'monsters' and natural wonders. All doctrine in the chapter can be used very successfully to summarise or expand students' present knowledge, as demonstrated in the project.

One of the most important elements in this chapter is that of wonder, awe, praise and thanksgiving in the face of the marvellous work of creation. If students are given the chance to present (in project form) those aspects of creation which most fill them with wonder and delight, then the Christian message of God's creation and our response of praise will be very relevant to the experience of students.

*Science and Scripture:* At this stage, the 'truthfulness' of the Scripture accounts bothers some students. 'Miss, Adam and Eve is all lies, now, isn't it?' is a comment sometimes heard. It is very important to avoid argument and confrontation on this issue. Some students are merely baiting the teacher, to try and get an excited response. Others may have a genuine question. The best way to respond is simply to remind students of what they have already learned:

(a) There is no contradiction between scientific and Scriptural accounts of Creation, since the purposes of the accounts are very different. The students are not being asked to accept the scientific understanding of the ancient Hebrews, but rather their religious insights. Similarly, many scientists with a great knowledge of the world in which we live are also faithful Christians.

(b) A story can contain many truths, even though all of the details may not be factual.

It is important not to try to force students to change their minds, or retract a statement. If we don't push them, they will often do so of their own accord. Losing face is one of the greatest threats at this age (or indeed at any age) and we must try to organise our programme so that this doesn't happen.

*Learning through pictures:* A visual image can help people to learn, and this is especially true for the less able. Many less able students are not capable of doing a project because of poor reading and writing skills, lack of resources at home, even poor motor-skills which makes cutting out a picture from a magazine a very difficult job. We would encourage the use of projects with as many students as possible, even if it takes them a long time and the results are not spectacular. However, with some students, it can be helpful to work directly from photographs, both those in the text and others presented by the teacher. Many beautiful posters are available free from travel agencies, embassies and development organisations. Many magazines have full-page colour prints which can be stuck onto cardboard or poster paper. The aim should be to stimulate students' imaginations and interest as much as possible. With a well-disciplined group, the pictures could be put up around the walls, and students could walk around as if in an art gallery, examining them. Later they could pick out their favourites and explain their choice. The teacher can present a simple work sheet asking students to explain what the pictures tell us about (a) God, (b) the world of nature, (c) people etc. Lastly, the class could read together part or all of the doctrine on pages 14 and 15.

Alternatively, each student could be given a picture. She or he must examine it and write/say (a) what is in the picture, (b) how many colours/different plants/different animals/other subjects are in the picture, (c) what words she/he would use to describe this picture,

(d) what does the picture tell you about God who created the scene, (e) compose a prayer to God, based on your picture.

If some students are finished before the others (if writing the answers), then they can be given another picture. If students are not asked to write, then they are given approximately five minutes to think (in silence) about their answers to the questions, and then call out their answers in turn to question 1; next the class goes on to question 2 etc. An overall summary can be made at the end about what they have learned.

*Psalms:* These can be used for meditation in the oratory, perhaps with suitable slides or a film sequence if available. Alternatively students could illustrate the Psalms using a series of drawings/pictures. (This might be given as an alternative choice for project.)

*Related themes:* God's love for us; created in God's image; stewardship.

## CHAPTER 4: I AM CREATED IN GOD'S IMAGE

*Aims of Lesson 4*
1. To teach students the concept of 'image'.
2. To explain what is meant by the doctrine that we are made in the image of God.

*Objectives of Lesson 4*
1. That students will be able to explain and give examples of the concept of 'image'.
2. That students will give examples to show how people can demonstrate that they are made in God's image.
3. That students will explore their own experience of being the image of God.

*Number of class periods required* 2

*Development of lesson*
1. Starter, first body of content, exercises, second body of content and second set of exercises.
2. Group work.

**Starter:** With many classes, the teacher will need to use recall and comprehension questions with the starter, to encourage students to work out logically the links between the photograph, cardiograph and the description of Jack.

**Sin:** You may wish to use additional exercises to emphasise the fact that we can choose not to reflect what God is like in our lives. This can be linked to conscience and sin. Students might act out two scenarios: (a) Where a person behaves as the image of God in a situation and (b) Where the same person in the same situation chooses not to behave as the image of God.

***Related themes:*** God's love for us; stewardship; freedom and responsibility; personal development.

## CHAPTER 5: MY RESPONSE TO GOD'S CREATION

*Aims of Lesson 5*
1. To explain what stewardship means.
2. To explain to students that they are called to be stewards.

*Objectives of Lesson 5*
1. That students will be able to explain what is meant by stewardship and will give examples of it.
2. That students will examine their own lives to see the ways in which they act as stewards, or how they could improve their stewardship.

*Number of class periods required* 1

**Stewardship:** Stewardship is a basic theme throughout *Believe the Good News.* When students have shown a thorough understanding of stewardship, and applied the concept to their relationship with their environment and with others, it could be useful to devote some extra class periods to researching and presenting the assignment, planning the action, or preparing and celebrating a prayer-service on stewardship.

**Starter:** The picture includes many things which are in some ways under the control of 13 to 14-year-olds, for example: people (especially family and friends, and the local community); buildings (both public and private); the countryside (litter, rules of safety etc.); trees; animals (can be expanded from the cows in the picture to include household pets); roads (and transport, to include the school bus where appropriate); the air — cigarette-smoke, aerosol sprays with CFCs etc.; telephone-boxes and other public utilities; walls (graffiti); water (water safety, litter etc.).

Some students may need to be given a few examples to get them started.

**Related themes:** Loving God and others; Creation; image of God; relationships; personal development.

## CHAPTER 6: HOW FREE AM I?

*Aims of Lesson 6*
1. To explain what freedom means.
2. To show different kinds of limitations to our freedom.
3. To show that some limitations have to be accepted, while others can be overcome.
4. To explain that we should use our freedom to show what God is like.

*Objectives of Lesson 6*
1. To give students an experience of freedom and limitation.
2. That students will explore their experiences of freedom and limitation.
3. That students will give examples to illustrate how they can use their freedom to show that they are made in the image of God.
4. That students will identify the different kinds of limitation which they experience.
5. That students will give examples to show how limitations can be accepted or overcome, thus enabling themselves to become better people.
6. That students will analyse how they use their day-to-day freedom by filling in and examining a Time-Chart.

*Number of class periods required* 3

*Development of lesson*
1. The game.
2. The questions on the game, the three blocks of content and the accompanying exercises.
3. The assignment and the accompanying questions.

**Freedom:** Freedom in human terms is always relative. It can be useful for students to give examples of 'complete' freedom and to give students the opportunity to analyse those examples. This will make it clear that absolute freedom is not possible. In every situation, outside of science fiction or fantasy, people have to eat, breathe and eventually die. This should be a 'discovery' for students, rather than a 'victory' for the teacher.

It might also be useful to examine situations in which people appear to be very unfree (prisoners, people in wheelchairs, etc.) and yet who *are* free in some very important ways. As the old hymn 'Faith of our Fathers' puts it (in a rather sexist way):
    'Our Fathers chained in prisons dark
    Were still in heart and conscience free.'

This is an aspect of freedom which some students find fascinating. There is scope here for a good project, using information from organisations for people who are disabled or from Amnesty International or any current 'human achievement' stories.

**Starter:** We would encourage the teacher to allow students to play the game if they want to. They are very quick at picking up the rules, since this type of game is very familiar to them. Some teachers are afraid that chaos will result from such an exercise. This is only likely if the class is not well prepared. All the rules for group work apply — indeed, the game should *only* be played with a class who work well in groups. The teacher is the arbitrator whose decision is final in all disputes. Students whose previous behaviour makes it seem likely that they will not be capable of taking part quietly in the game can, if there are not too many of them, be given 'special' functions. They can be 'supervisors', making sure everyone keeps the rules; they can design their own freedom game, perhaps situated in outer space; or they could do another simple exercise, such as designing/colouring in a poster on freedom.

Have a few practice runs first, before playing the game in earnest, to sort out any problems. Remember to present the game as entertainment rather than as a learning exercise, and a special treat for well-behaved students, rather than a desperate attempt to win the attention of unruly ones!

*Obstacles:* These are designed to highlight (albeit in an artificial way) the limitations imposed on people by their natural environment, their physical needs, their personal inadequacies and failings, the actions (both good and bad) of other people, and their personal decision or choice to limit themselves for the good of others. When the students have been given the chance to talk about their experience of the game, the teacher should start the exploration of the 'learning' aspect of the game by asking the questions (page 26). Question 6 is designed to elicit from the students their understanding of freedom and limitations, enriched by playing the game. Exercise 2 (page 26), 'What do you do that limits the freedom of other people?' should be approached from both the positive and the negative points of view. For example, if I vandalise a telephone box, I prevent people using the phone. When I am babysitting, I don't allow the children to play with knives.

Exercise 3 (page 27), 'Have you ever overcome a limitation, weakness or other difficulty?' will probably be a private exercise, not for reading out, with most groups of students.

*Assignment:* Most students enjoy this type of activity, though the less able may need very close supervision. With the less able it can be good to decide as a class on the categories to be included, e.g. (a) sleeping, (b) at school, (c) eating/meal-times, (d) praying, (e) leisure/free time, (f) jobs at home. Travel may also be included if it is a big part of the students' day. The teacher may think it wise to give the students ready-made charts with the hours marked around the circumference, so that they only have to divide them up between the different categories. Any activity like this needs to be strongly reinforced, especially with less able students. If the Time-Charts are done on posters or sheets of paper, they should be displayed on the wall with the student's name clearly visible. If they are in the student's copy, the teacher should make a personal written comment beside each student's work, praising whatever can be praised.

After the Time-Chart has been completed, ask the better able students to evaluate how well they are using their freedom; what main limitations they experience as indicated by their charts; and how they might spend time to use their freedom in a better way.

*Discussion:* 'Freedom is more than doing what you want.' Having studied the chapter, students will be aware of the Christian concept of freedom, a gift to be used to do what God wants of us: that we be loving, caring stewards. Not all students may agree with the Christian

message. However, a discussion is a good opportunity for the teacher to evaluate the learning that has taken place.
*Related themes:* Making choices; rules; conscience; decision-making; personal development; sin and reconciliation.

## CHAPTER 7: MEETING GOD

*Aims of Lesson 7*
1. To remind students that God is always with us.
2. To show that we have to respond to God freely and give time to our relationship with God.

Objectives of Lesson 7
1. That students will explore the experience of being aware of God.
2. That they will identify the ways in which they can meet God.

*Number of class periods required* 1

*Prayer:* From the beginning of the year it is good to give students the opportunity to pray together using prayer-services and quiet meditation or oratory experiences. This introductory chapter is designed to help students think about their relationship with God, and how God is with them through people and events. When they have looked at these areas, it might be good to examine and explore more specifically the area of prayer. The following 'Oratory' or meditation-type experience of prayer is usually very successful with students, especially if you are willing to be patient and give plenty of time for the giggles etc. to subside. If this exercise must be done in the students' own classroom, then try to have the room darkened; black bags over the windows might help. Use any stimulus which will raise the experience from that of the everyday classroom. Incense sticks, perfumed candles and flowers, as well as music, can all help to promote a good atmosphere. If at all possible, prepare the room before the students enter it, and control the group well as they enter.
1. Students enter the room quietly and (if possible) sit on the floor.
2. Explain quietly, when there is complete silence, what will be happening, e.g. a time of stillness, a special experience, no talking.
3. Students sit or lie still, eyes closed, in a physically correct manner, so that they will not fidget.
4. Play some appropriate non-intrusive music moderately loud for a minute or two, then turn it down so that it is just audible.
5. Lead students through a relaxation exercise lasting for a minimum of five minutes.
6. Lead students through a breathing exercise for five minutes.
7. Bring students on a spirit journey. They imagine they are somewhere else, they go on a journey, they reach a special place, they meet someone. It is Jesus. He speaks to them; they speak to him. Allow a period of silence. They say goodbye to Jesus, they

leave the special place, they retrace their journey (exactly the same as they took before), they arrive back at their starting point. Then they realise that they are in the 'oratory' (or wherever) (15 minutes).
8. Lead students through an exercise in awareness of their body (3-5 minutes).
9. Allow students to open their eyes. Encourage them to stay as they are for a few moments.

For a very giddy group, a 10-minute shortened version may be more appropriate. In the classroom, some students relax better resting their head on their arms on top of the desk or table.

Ordinary prayer-services should also be planned and celebrated by students throughout the year. The guidelines in Chapter 44 may prove helpful here.

*Related themes:* Prayer; worship; sacraments; personal development; God's presence; God's call and my response; the Liturgical Year.

## CHAPTER 8: FREE TO CHOOSE

*Aims of Lesson 8*
1. To teach the concept of conscience.
2. To explain what is meant by the term 'informed conscience'.
3. To show that when we freely follow our conscience, we are showing that we are the image of God.

*Objectives of Lesson 8*
1. That students will explain and give examples of using their conscience and following their conscience.
2. That students will explore the experience of using their conscience and evaluate the place conscience has in their everyday choices.
3. That students will use Scripture and the teaching of the Church to inform their conscience.
4. That they will give examples to demonstrate how they can show they are made in the image of God by following their conscience.

*Number of class periods required* 3

*Development of lesson*
1. Starter and questions, first block of content, first set of exercises, group work.
2. Story of John, questions, next block of content, exercises, definition of informed conscience.
3. Block of content starting 'God always helps...' to end of chapter.

**Conscience:** This can be a very satisfying concept to teach, because most students are well able to make the leap from 'the little voice inside' to a capacity to judge, which is a gift from God. It is very important to give enough time to exploring the starter stories. It is possible you will not get to the group work in the first class, if the students are working well on the starter.

Make sure that students understand the term 'capacity'. It has overtones of ability, but with potential for greater development. A capacity is a power — students should be able to give examples of other capacities, and to compare and contrast them with conscience.

Some less able students will need to examine several examples to differentiate between 'using' and 'following' conscience. This is basically the difference between 'knowing' and 'doing'.

*Group work:* This exercise may be too difficult for the less able to do on their own in groups. In this case it can be done as a whole class exercise, led by the teacher.

*Informed conscience:* Less able students may need to tackle this at a later stage in the programme, to avoid giving them too much new material at once on the same theme.

*Examination of conscience:* You may wish to introduce or remind students at this stage of the value and purpose of examining one's conscience. This might most fruitfully be done in an oratory lesson.

*Related themes:* Making choices; sin and reconciliation; image of God; stewardship; freedom; decision-making.

## CHAPTER 9: MAKING DECISIONS

*Aims of Lesson 9*
1. To explain that we need others to help us make important decisions.
2. To outline a possible decision-making process.

*Objectives of Lesson 9*
1. That students will examine how they go about making decisions.
2. That they will give examples showing how other people can help them to make decisions.
3. That they will apply the decision-making process to a given situation.

*Number of class periods required* 2

*Development of lesson*
1. Starter, questions, first block of content, exercises.
2. Guidelines on making a decision, to the end of the chapter.

*Decision-making:* The focus of the chapter is 'informed decision-making'. This develops the theme of the informed conscience, and expands the idea of judgment between a right and wrong action to the judgment of an overall situation which is more complex, and in which 'rights and wrongs' are less clear cut. It is good to encourage students to see why the informed conscience, although the final arbiter, is not the only element to consider when making a decision. Other elements guide and inform conscience. At this age, students' lack of experience and knowledge may lead to their 'conscience' decisions being in opposition to the basic Christian message. While not in any way compromising Christian truth, we must encourage students to find this truth in their experience, rather than simply rejecting their immature conclusions. It is very helpful to give examples which do not threaten students, but which highlight the guidance needed by young people. For example, a student wants to change schools because he doesn't like one of his teachers; a teenager refuses to talk to her sister — even though it is weeks since they had a row — because she can't forgive her. The purpose here is to encourage students seriously to reconsider their decisions, if their conscience runs contrary to the Christian message. To this end, the examples should show that conscience can benefit from the guidance of others. The guidelines show where to look for this guidance.

*Related themes:* Making choices, conscience; sin and reconciliation; stewardship; freedom; image of God.

## UNIT II: RELATIONSHIPS
## CHAPTER 10: ADOLESCENCE

*Aims of Lesson 10*
1. To introduce the topic of early adolescence.
2. To present the following characteristics of early adolescence to the students: (a) the change in relationships; (b) the growing need for independence of thought and action; (c) the need to make important personal decisions.
3. To present adolescence as a part of God's loving plan.

*Objectives of Lesson 10*
1. That students will explore the difficulties and challenges of adolescent relationships with adults.
2. That students will explore briefly their experience of thinking about and making decisions for themselves.

*Number of class periods required* 1

***Adolescence:*** Neither Chapter 10 nor Chapter 11 ('Growing Up') tries to give a comprehensive account of adolescence. However, these chapters can be used as a starting point for such a study. Alternatively, they could be used as a conclusion, since they pick up the main points which would be covered, and give students the opportunity to see the significance of adolescence in Christian terms.

***Teacher-student relationships:*** It is important not to dodge the issue of teacher-student relationships in school. It is not helpful to have students mentioning teachers by name and giving chapter and verse of their faults and failings. It is, however, possible to approach the topic in an objective manner. General comments and questions can be put forward and discussed in class. It is no harm to remind students of the legal meaning of slander, just in case! The teacher should make his/her position perfectly clear — the teacher is a member of the teaching staff with loyalty to colleagues and management. At the same time, the teacher will not pretend that all teacher-student relationships are perfect, or that every problem is caused by a student. The teacher must make it clear that the purpose of discussing teacher/student relationships in religion class is to try and improve them, and not to indulge in 'teacher-bashing' and gossip. Specific problems must be dealt with privately. General topics which can be usefully aired include politeness between teachers and students ('He shouts at me but if I shout at him I get detention'); punctuality for lessons and other appointments in school; what to do if you think a teacher doesn't like you; what to do if you dislike a teacher; 'unfair' punishment; and being picked on in class.

All problems will not be solved by class discussion, but students can be encouraged to approach problems in a helpful way. Firstly, they can try to understand why the problem has arisen. This often involves coming to terms with the basic facts of human relationships, the question of authority and the fact of adolescence. Many students may realise for the first time that they would have had no problem two years ago with a situation which is now intolerable to them.

Secondly, they can decide how to behave now that the problem is there. They can be given strategies for avoiding confrontation (e.g. not talking out of turn, slouching or showing contempt for the teacher by their physical comportment). Many students react very favourably to this aspect of control. Often they get a feeling of power by deliberately annoying a teacher. Now they can see the reverse use of power in operation, in the interest of better relationships.

Thirdly, they can be given strategies for approaching the teacher or teachers with whom they have a problem, to try and improve the situation. For example, shouting to a teacher in the middle of class that you don't understand a word of what is going on, and what is she going to do about it, is not a helpful strategy. It is better to make an appointment to see the teacher alone, or with a parent/guardian, after school and explain your difficulties. Many students are surprised to learn that teachers can be flattered to be asked for help. Politeness towards a teacher is always helpful, and costs nothing but self-control. Really serious problems should be discussed at home and/or with a tutor or member of the school management. Presenting your point of view in a calm, non-judgmental way is essential if you wish to be taken seriously.

Role-plays can be very helpful here. It is often best if the teacher takes the part of the adult in the role-play.

*Related themes:* Personal development; decision-making; freedom; relationships; God's love.

# CHAPTER 11: GROWING UP

*Aims of Lesson 11*
1. To outline the stages of human growth in terms of physical, emotional, mental, social and spiritual development.
2. To show that, as people grow older, they can often choose whether or not to co-operate with God's plan for their development.
3. To introduce the idea of death as a normal event in human development.

*Objectives of Lesson 11*
1. That students will be able to identify the main stages of human development, and the principal changes which take place in each stage.
2. That students will explore their own experience of growing up and give examples of the changes and developments that are taking place in their present lives.
3. That students will be able to explain how death leads to new life.

*Number of class periods required* 2-3

*Development of lesson*
1. Starter, questions, first block of content (pages 48 to 55).
2-3. Group work to the end of the chapter.

**Starter:** Less able students might find so much information confusing. In this case it might be helpful for the whole class to examine each of the pictures in turn, and write a brief summary about the stage of human development represented. There is no need to divide this summary into separate categories. The teacher should guide the students into consideration of, 'What kinds of things can the people in this photograph do that the people in the previous photographs could not do?', 'What different interests would they have?' etc.

**Growth and development:** It is important to note that each individual grows and develops at a unique pace that is right for him/her. Some people begin puberty at 10 years of age, others experience puberty at 15 or 16. Girls tend to mature at a faster rate than boys. It is vital to emphasise that variation is the norm.

**Related themes:** Adolescence; death and eternal life; freedom; stewardship.

# CHAPTER 12: FAMILY

*Aims of Lesson 12*
1. To focus on relationships within the family, and to show how they can grow and develop during the adolescence of one or more members.
2. To show that all families can have problems.
3. To give a Scriptural background to the issues which arise in family life.

*Objectives of Lesson 12*
1. That students will explore the advantages and disadvantages of family life during adolescence.
2. That they will come to a greater understanding and awareness of the problems of parents.
3. That they will apply a message from Scripture to modern family life.

*Number of class periods required* 3-4

*Development of lesson*
1. Starter, questions.
2-3. Content (page 58), exercises and content (pages 59-60).
3-4. Group work.

**Starter:** It is important to give enough time to the starter, and in particular to allow students to set their own agenda with question 4.
**Content:** With less able students it is essential to choose appropriate content from the chapter. It is more important to address student needs than to read every sentence in the text. The teacher might focus on the coloured block of content (page 58), having done the starter, and then go on to the exercises at the top of page 59.

Many less able students enjoy Scripture work, but it would be good to work on the exercises as a class, or perhaps in groups. Some students may need to spend one or two classes on this topic, and then take a break to do something else before coming back to it again.
**Group work:** This exercise can work very well. A variation is to ask some groups to be the parents of Kevin, and others to be Kevin — what should he do now? After the presentations, two students could role-play a scene between Kevin and a parent on the following day. (In many schools, it may be appropriate to replace Kevin with Annette!)
**Related themes:** Personal development; relationships; stewardship; learning from Scripture; adolescence.

## CHAPTER 13: FRIENDSHIP

*Aims of Lessons 13*
1. To show why we need friends.
2. To introduce the idea of peer-groups.
3. To explain the Christian message about friendship.

*Objectives of Lesson 13*
1. That students will analyse their experience of friendship.
2. That students will evaluate the importance of friendship in their lives.
3. That students will have the opportunity to reflect on and discuss peer-group pressure.
4. That students will apply the message of Scripture to their own friendships.

*Number of class periods required* 2-3

*Development of lesson*
1. Starter, questions, content and exercises (page 62).
2. Exercises (page 63). (Discussion on peer-group pressure optional)
3. Content (page 63), exercises (page 64).

**Cartoon:** As your students will no doubt point out, the dog in the cartoon is called Snoopy, not Peanuts!

**Friendship:** At this stage many students are beginning to move away from the 'one best friend' syndrome. Others cling closely to the best friend. Still others appear to be loners, sitting by themselves if possible, as if they fear rejection if they sit beside someone. Some students have drifted into gangs or groups in many of which there is a strongly established pecking order. The precise mix of any of these patterns in any particular class will determine the teacher's approach to this topic. One thing all the students have in common is a need to belong and be accepted. For some of them, this need is met outside of the class grouping they happen to be in for religious education, and so it can be very useful to do a confidential questionnaire with students before using the text. The questions might include

(1) If you had an important secret, would you tell it to (a) your family, (b) one good friend, (c) a small group of friends, (d) anyone you know, (e) no-one?
(2) Do you see your best friend(s) (a) several times a day, (b) once a day, (c) once a week, (d) less often?
(3) Would you like to have (a) more friends, (b) fewer friends, (c) one best friend, (d) exactly the same friends as you have now?

The results of the survey can be given in general terms to the class, in such a way that no one could possibly be identified. For example, if there is an obviously lonely and isolated person in the class, and one questionnaire is returned which states that the person is lonely and has no friends, it would obviously be harmful to mention that 'one person feels she or he has no friend'. However, if several people say they would like more friends, this can be made public.

**Peer-group pressure:** If this issue arises and seems to be important to the group, it would be useful to give some time to either a written exercise, group-work or a discussion on the topic. The important thing is not to isolate named individuals as causing the problem. It is better to encourage students to examine their own response to peer-pressure and to help them work out strategies for dealing with it. Again, this is largely a consciousness-raising exercise. Many students will freely admit to being strongly influenced by their peers, disliking this in themselves, but recognising that they are not yet strong enough to reject it completely. As a student said on one occasion, 'Miss, we'll all agree to anything when we're in here; it all makes sense and we know what we *should* do. But when we get out there, we're going to be just as bad as the rest of them, because we haven't got the guts to stand on our own two feet.' This was in relation to smoking.

We do have to reassure students that it might take a long time before their real selves catch up with their ideal images. Students can easily become discouraged if impossible goals are set. The teacher can help by giving guidelines on how to take 'the single step'. 'If you feel you have to smoke, use bad language or be rude in order to be popular, even though you do not *want* to do these things, then decide on *one* action which you could take, the first step towards getting out of this situation. Then you can try the second step, and so on.' These steps can be worked out by the student with guidance from the teacher. The 'one day at a time' rule, or even one hour at a time, can be very helpful. The most important step has already been taken when someone decides she or he no longer wishes to be pressurised into doing something wrong or harmful.

***Related themes:*** Stewardship; relationships; freedom; learning from Scripture; personal development.

## CHAPTER 14: GOD'S CALL AND MY RESPONSE

*Aims of Lesson 14*
1. To present the story of Jonah as one of call and response.
2. To explain the different ways in which God calls us to stewardship of ourselves, other people, the environment, and our relationship with God.
3. To show that following or answering God's call involves taking a risk.

*Objectives of Lesson 14*
1. That students will explore the story of Jonah, and explain what meaning it has for them.
2. That students will examine their experiences of being called by God and the consequences of that call.

*Number of class periods required* 1-2

***The story of Jonah:*** It would be useful to do some background reading on this story, so that you will feel more comfortable presenting it to students. A good introduction can be found in Fr William Riley's book, *The Bible Group: An Owner's Manual,* Veritas Publications 1983.

***God's call:*** You may wish to give students an opportunity to consider the consequences of ignoring God's call on a long-term basis. The theme of sin and reconciliation is linked to that of God's call. 'If I get into the habit of ignoring God's call to love and care for myself and others, I will become a weaker person, less able to resist the temptation of sin.'

***Related themes:*** Prayer and worship; God's love for me; vocation; sin and reconciliation; stewardship.

# CHAPTER 15: BEING A STEWARD TO MYSELF

*Aims of Lesson 15*
1. To show that looking after self is an important part of being a steward.
2. To build up students' self-esteem and self-respect.

*Objectives of Lesson 15*
1. That students will analyse their experience of being a steward to themselves.
2. That they will give examples of how they can improve in this stewardship.

*Number of class periods required* 1-2

**Starter:** When students have completed this exercise, it can be very useful to get their reactions to it. What is their opinion of the issues raised? Do they agree with the conclusions (i.e. mostly a's and b's means one is looking after oneself well)? Do they consider looking after oneself to be selfish? Where would they draw the line between 'looking after No.1' and loving self? What are the long-term consequences of neglecting one's health, mind etc.?
***Related themes:*** Personal development; stewardship.

# UNIT III: RELATIONSHIPS IN TROUBLE
# CHAPTER 16: SIN

*Aims of Lesson 16*
1. To develop the students' concept of sin, in the context of stewardship.
2. To explain what is meant by mortal and venial sin.

*Objectives of Lesson 16*
1. That students will be able to explain and give examples of sin.
2. That students will be able to differentiate between mortal and venial sin.
3. That students will explore their experience of sin and sinfulness.

*Number of class periods required* 2-3

*Development of lesson*
1. Starter and questions.
2. Content and exercises (pages 81 and 82).
3. Content and assignment. (Possibly an oratory class, also using the reflection, action, song and prayer.)

**Starter:** Aaron's story is very long, but worthwhile if approached in the right way. Unless students are excellent readers (members of the drama society or public speakers) the teacher should read the story. Depending on the class, this can be done in the classroom or in the oratory. If in the oratory, then it can be read by the teacher as part of a meditation exercise. In this case, students do not have their books open. It might be useful to have the students look up the story of the Prodigal Son, Luke 15:11-32 (on which the story of Aaron is based) and compare and contrast it with the story of Aaron. Then they might make up their own 'modern version'.

*Content:* Again, the content must be carefully selected to suit less able students. A good analysis of Aaron's story is the basis for the quality of learning to be expected. The teacher might focus on the definition of sin (second highlighted passage page 81) and explain in her or his own words the meaning of mortal and venial sin, using some of the examples in the textbook.

For more able students, examples could be given and analysed, to work out clearly the differences between venial and mortal sin. For example, if I attack someone and rob him, because the gang say they will beat me up if I don't, am I freely and deliberately committing a mortal sin? The aim here is not to encourage scrupulousness, but rather to help students see the importance of thinking about actions beforehand, using conscience and trying to do what is right and loving. This should also highlight God's love and concern. God takes our intentions into account and judges the heart. At the same time, examining examples which are realistic enables students to develop an awareness of what sin really means.

*Related themes:* Freedom; stewardship; conscience; reconciliation; the Sacrament of Reconciliation.

## CHAPTER 17: THE BREAKDOWN OF RELATIONSHIPS

*Aims of Lesson 17*
1. To show that sin harms our relationships with each other, our world and God.
2. To present the story of Adam and Eve as a Scripture story which has a meaning for our lives today.

*Objectives of Lesson 17*
1. That students will be able to explain the message or meaning in the story of Adam and Eve's sin.
2. That students will examine their experience of sin and note the effects that sin has on relationships.

*Number of class periods required* 1

*Starter:* This story is a good one to act out or mime. Some students may feel that God was unfair — shouldn't Adam and Eve have been given another chance? Remind students that this is not a historical

account, but a story which explains what sin is and what its consequences are. God's words to the snake and to the sinful pair are words of punishment, but it is a punishment brought about by the sinners themselves. Ask students to think of a few examples of people who suffer because of their sin, even though they are not 'caught' or 'punished' by another person: someone who tells lies and lives in dread of being found out; someone who is nasty and rude and so ends up with no friends etc.
*Related themes:* Sin and reconciliation; relationships; conscience.

## CHAPTER 18: REBUILDING BROKEN RELATIONSHIPS

*Aims of Lesson 18*
1. To explain the steps that lead to reconciliation.
2. To show that through the Sacrament of Reconciliation we can become reconciled with God and with the rest of the Christian community.
3. To explain that confession of sins is an important part of reconciliation.

*Objectives of Lesson 18*
1. That students will be able to describe and explain the steps that lead to reconciliation.
2. That students will give examples to show how they can build up relationships through the Sacrament of Reconciliation.
3. That the students will be able to explain the value of confessing or saying what they have done wrong, as a step in reconciliation.

*Number of class periods required* 2

*Development of lesson*
1. Starter, questions, first block of content and exercises (page 90).
2. From the assignment to the end of the chapter.

**Starter:** It might be useful to allow students to make up their own 'typical letters' to a problem page, and then base the exercises and questions on those letters.
**Content:** It is important to choose the content carefully from this chapter. Many students who are less able cannot remember more than two or three points per lesson, so plan accordingly. Each separate paragraph makes a different, though related point. Give students plenty of opportunities to give examples illustrating each point as it is made, and/or to comment on the issue from their own experience. Students do not have to study every paragraph in depth in order to achieve the objectives and aims.
**Project:** This can be done as an alternative starter, especially with a more able group. Students can then apply the steps towards reconciliation to the examples they have researched, to see how they are

being applied. You might encourage them to differentiate between (a) reconciling relationships which have broken down and (b) building up relationships which have not broken down, but which need improvement.

*Related themes:* Sin and reconciliation; stewardship; conscience; relationships; Sacrament of Reconciliation; God's call and my response.

## CHAPTER 19: EVIL AND SUFFERING

*Aims of Lesson 19*
1. To explain what is meant by evil.
2. To show that evil causes many kinds of suffering.
3. To show that evil takes away our freedom in some way.
4. To explain that some forms of suffering have an obvious purpose.
5. To present the problem of suffering which appears to have no purpose.
6. To show that good things can happen during a time of suffering.
7. To explain that God can bring new life and hope out of terrible suffering.

*Objectives of Lesson 19*
1. That students will identify human evil as the cause of many kinds of suffering.
2. That students will examine briefly how they have suffered because of evil.
3. That students will explore their experience of losing freedom because of sin and evil.
4. That students will examine the good and bad elements which are present in a time of suffering.
5. That students will be able to explain the Christian understanding of suffering and its meaning, and will apply this message to their everyday lives using examples.

*Number of class periods required* 2-3

*Development of lesson*
1. Starter, questions, content and exercises (page 94).
2-3. From the content (page 95) to the end of the chapter.

**Evil and suffering:** Both topics are dealt with together because of their close relationship. They are two of the greatest mysteries in human life. Even many committed and informed Christians have great difficulty in this area, which can test one's faith to its limits.

It is vital to approach these topics cautiously with students, measuring their reactions as you go along. It is good to respond to their questions, and especially to give them the Christian message of God's love and presence in the midst of suffering, but we must be careful not to burden them with fear and anxiety. Most students will be able to study and benefit from all of the material in this chapter, but the large number of aims and objectives should make it easy for the teacher to choose (and omit) material for less able students. The general guideline is to allow students to explore and explain their present experience and understanding, and then give them one or two ideas to enrich their understanding.

*Monsters and nightmares:* You may find that some students' understanding of the term 'evil' has been largely informed by horror movies and creepy tales. Many 14- and even 15-year-olds are remarkably naive and innocent, and genuinely believe in 'demons of the deep' which have nothing to do with the Christian understanding of evil. Christians believe in evil, but this has nothing to do with the kind of highly-coloured nonsense which appears on our television and cinema screens.

Students should be encouraged to see evil for what it is: drab and miserable, rather than entertaining and exciting. Exorcisms are rare: poverty, pain and sorrow are very common. Allow students to work off steam in relation to 'the horrors', try to encourage a healthy scepticism, and focus the lesson on the realities of their own experience.

*Related themes:* Sin; relationships; Jesus' death and resurrection; freedom.

## CHAPTER 20: DEATH AND ETERNAL LIFE

*Aims of Lesson 20*
1. To explain that death is a natural part of life.
2. To explain what Jesus meant when he asked us to die ourselves so that we can really live.
3. To show that physical death leads to eternal life for Jesus' faithful followers.
4. To help students reflect on the fact that they will die.

*Objectives of Lesson 20*
1. That students will explore their understanding of and feelings about death and life after death.
2. That students will give examples to show that death leads to new life.
3. That students will explore what the Scriptures tell us about life after death.
4. That students will have the opportunity to think about the fact of their own death, and come to terms in some way with the impact of this reality.

*Number of class periods required* 2-3

*Development of lesson*
1. Starter, group work.
2-3. Content (page 100) to the end of the chapter.

***Death:*** We must be sensitive when approaching this topic. It is important to know beforehand if any of the students has experienced the death of a close relative or friend. The classroom is not the place for bereavement counselling and it is not wise to bring up issues which can have no satisfactory resolution in this setting. You may wish to use an alternative starter with some groups; the story of an old person dying peacefully surrounded by family and friends at the end of a long and happy life would be useful in some instances. The dying person should be presented as full of hope, and looking forward to meeting friends and family already deceased.

Another useful starter might be the story of the seed. Left on the shelf, it lived for years, never changing, always waiting. Then it is planted, thrown into the earth and it dies, decays. But from the decayed seed comes a beautiful new plant, with new seeds for future growth. This is one of the best metaphors for the resurrection, especially for the idea of being 'the same but different' after the resurrection.

With some groups, an oratory class might be a good way to introduce the topic, with gentle meditation, and a reminder that all our loved ones who are dead are now with God, and looking forward to being united with us again in heaven.

In our society, death can be 'invisible', so it can be good to give students an opportunity to think about death, and suggest ways of coping with the idea. Unfortunately, for some of us, death by violence is an ever-present fact of life. Death as a result of evil is very hard to come to terms with, and should be approached sensitively in the context of evil and suffering, and the call to reconciliation.

***Related themes:*** Jesus' death and resurrection; suffering and evil; sin and reconciliation; relationships; God's loving call.

## UNIT IV: SCRIPTURE
## CHAPTER 21: THE HISTORY OF SALVATION

*Aims of Lesson 21*
1. To teach students the concept of faithfulness.
2. To show that the history of salvation is the story of God's relationship with and faithfulness to the people.
3. To explain the meaning of Covenant.
4. To enrich the students' understanding of the Ten Commandments as part of a Covenant relationship.

*Objectives of Lesson 21*
1. That students will explore their experience of faithfulness, and give examples.
2. That students will be able to explain the meaning and significance of Covenant.
3. That students will apply the Commandments to their everyday lives.
4. That students will examine some of the Scripture stories which are part of the history of salvation.

*Number of class periods required* 4-5

*Development of lesson*
1. Starter, questions and first block of content (page 110).
2-3. Exercises and content (pages 110-112) and exercises (page 113).
4. Time-line and exercises.
5. Group work.

**Covenant:** Covenant faithfulness is the most important aspect of this chapter. Salvation means that God offers us a loving relationship with Him and with each other. The Covenant at Mount Sinai was a very important step in the history of salvation. The Covenant sealed by Jesus' blood on the cross is the central tenet of our faith. Therefore it is vital that all students should have some understanding of Covenant and its implications. In this context, the Ten Commandments are the hallmarks of our faithfulness to God, and Jesus' command that we love one another is the basis of our faithfulness to God in the new Covenant.
**Related themes:** Jesus' death and resurrection; Exodus; freedom; relationships; God's loving call.

## CHAPTER 22: EXODUS

*Aims of Lesson 22*
1. To teach the Exodus story, as one of God's love and faithfulness for all people, past and present.
2. To explain that becoming free is a long and difficult struggle, made possible only with God's help.

*Objectives of Lesson 22*
1. That students will explore the Exodus story, and explain the messages or meanings it has for them.
2. That students will identify and give examples of the difficulties involved in becoming a free person.

*Number of class periods required* 3

*Development of lesson*
1. Starter and questions.
2. Content (page 126), exercises (page 127).
3. Content (pages 127 and 128) and exercises (page 128).

**Starter:** The story is very long and should be read by the teacher. An oratory class would be a good setting. If the teacher feels a certain class would enjoy the story better in 'serial' form, doing short exercises based on the text after each section, then the story could be divided as follows:
 (a) Rameses (pages 116-18) to '...a nightmare for them'.
 (b) Moses (pages 118-19) to '...free them from their misery'.
 (c) Pharaoh (pages 119-20) to '...it will be the worse for you'.

(d) The Plagues (pages 120-22) to '...and would not give in'.
(e) The First Passover (page 122) to '...joys and dangers of freedom'.
(f) The Red Sea (pages 122-23).
(g) Freedom (pages 124-25) to '...complaining like this'.
(h) The Promised Land (page 125).

*Action:* It would be very beneficial, in terms of learning, to give students time to organise this activity. It can be daunting with less able students, who need so much teacher input, but they are the ones who benefit most from the achievement. The class might aim to be less ambitious — organise an Exodus day or lunch-hour, instead of a week, or do a project incorporating some suggestions in the text. Sometimes this action can work well if a year group works together, each taking responsibility for a different aspect. Less able students should be given achievable but high-profile roles, e.g. contacting, welcoming and introducing speakers; presenting the story of Exodus in project or drama form to the school; or making posters to advertise activities to take place.

*Related themes:* Freedom; God's love for us; Jesus' death and resurrection.

## CHAPTER 23: THE GOSPELS

*Aims of Lesson 23*
1. To explain briefly the background to the Gospels and why they were written.
2. To give a brief introduction to each of the evangelists.

*Objectives of Lesson 23*
1. That students will be able to give examples from their own experience to show how there can be many truthful but different versions of the same event.
2. That students will be able to describe briefly the main themes in each of the four gospels.
3. That students will explore the similarities and differences in the way Matthew, Mark and Luke present the story of Jesus healing a leper.

*Number of class periods required* 2

*Development of lesson*
1. Starter, questions, content and exercises (page 131) and the first block of content and questions (page 132).
2. Content on the evangelists (pages 132-33) and exercises (page 134).

**The Gospels:** Good background information can be found in *The Teachers' Source Book of the Bible,* editor Robert C. Walton, S.C.M. Press Ltd. With more able students, the teacher might stress the amount of research which has been done on the Gospels and indeed on the

whole of the Scriptures. Some classes might like to do a project on 'The Dead Sea Scrolls', or techniques used to analyse old documents. This information is readily available in encyclopedias.
**Related themes:** Jesus; salvation history.

## CHAPTER 24: JESUS

*Aims of Lesson 24*
1. To explain the different kinds of power people have, and the different ways of using power.
2. To present the story of Jesus' baptism, and his period of temptation in the desert, as a time of decision for Jesus.
3. To explain that the only good way to use power is to do what God wants.

*Objectives of Lesson 24*
1. That students will explore different kinds of power which they and other people have.
2. That students will examine the story of Jesus' baptism and temptation and see what message or meaning it has for them.
3. That students will give examples to show how they can use their power as Jesus did, to love others and follow God's plan.

*Number of class periods required* 1-2

**Power:** Give students an opportunity to link the notion of power to the concepts of image and stewardship. One of the most radical aspects of Jesus' message is his insistence on the loving use of power, turning the other cheek, forgiving and not seeking revenge. Many students of 13 or 14 are outraged by this message. The important thing here is not to 'convince' them that Jesus is right, but allow them to see through their own examples that he is right. Many of them will not like what they see. It can be very useful to allow them to discuss the topic suggested at the end of the chapter, a few days after the lesson, but not formally linked with it. This gives the teacher a chance to see what students have gained from their lesson on power.
**Related themes:** Stewardship; image of God; relationships; Jesus; salvation history.

## CHAPTER 25: IMAGES OF JESUS

*Aims of Lesson 25*
1. To enable students to discover the kind of person Jesus is.
2. To explain the titles used for Jesus in the synoptic Gospels.

*Objectives of Lesson 25*
1. That students will examine and identify the images of Jesus presented in the synoptic Gospels.

2. That students will be able to explain, in their own words, the significance of titles given to Jesus in the synoptic Gospels.

*Number of class periods required* 1-2

***Starter:*** Less able groups will need to do this starter as a class, with plenty of help and direction from the teacher.
***Assignment:*** This can be used as an alternative starter. When students have studied the content, they can go back and re-evaluate their account of Jesus' visit in light of what they have learned.
***Related themes:*** Salvation history; the Gospels; suffering; image; stewardship; relationships.

## CHAPTER 26: JESUS' DEATH AND RESURRECTION

*Aims of Lesson 26*
1. To explain what is meant by the terms 'salvation' and 'saviour'.
2. To show that Jesus is the only true saviour.
3. To explain that salvation is a gift, which we must choose to accept or reject.
4. To explain the significance of the resurrection in terms of salvation.
5. To show that accepting God's gift of salvation can involve suffering.

*Objectives of Lesson 26*
1. That students will explore their understanding of what a saviour is, and why people need to be saved.
2. That students will be able to explain the Christian meaning of the term 'salvation', and give examples to show ways in which this salvation is needed.
3. That students will identify ways in which Jesus offered salvation to the people he met.
4. That students will be able to explain in their own words the significance of Jesus' death and resurrection for us today.

*Number of class periods required* 2-3

*Development of lesson*
1. Starter, questions, first block of content and exercises (page 143).
2. Content at bottom of page 143, and top of page 144; exercises (page 144).
3. Second block of content (page 144); exercises and content (page 145).

***The good news:*** The doctrine in this chapter is the central core of the Christian message. As St Paul tells us, 'If Christ is not risen, then our faith is vain.' This is an important chapter to plan and implement carefully. It gathers together the basic themes introduced in Units I to III; God's love and care for us; God's generosity in offering us salvation; sin and reconciliation; God's call to freedom and loving relationships with one another as God's children; the meaning of suffering. This chapter is also the foundation for the topics of Eucharist and thanksgiving, sacrifice, and Easter.

For less able students, it is better to attempt one objective at a time, preferably in the context of some of the other themes in the programme. For example, when doing the topic of 'God's call and my response' (Chapter 14), students might explore the way in which God calls them through Jesus to become children of God. Jesus made this possible for us by dying and rising from the dead.

**Related themes:** As above.

## UNIT V: SACRAMENTS
## CHAPTER 27: SIGNS AND SYMBOLS

*Aims of Lesson 27*
1. To revise and expand the students' understanding of signs and symbols.
2. To show the need for symbolic language in everyday life.
3. To revise the ways in which signs and symbols are important to Christians.
4. To explain and give examples of sacramentals.

*Objectives of Lesson 27*
1. That students will give examples of signs and symbols.
2. That students will explore their use and understanding of sacramentals.
3. That students will give examples to show that signs and symbols help us to communicate with God.

*Number of class periods required* 2-3

*Development of lesson*
1. Starter, questions, first block of content, first set of exercises.
2. Second block of content, exercises, examples of sacramentals and exercises (page 150).
3. Group work.

**Starter:** This exercise is *meant* to be almost impossible! It tries to give students an experience of needing symbolic language to describe what cannot ever be fully described, but only experienced. Some students could be chosen as judges, and the rest of the class divided into teams. Each team gets marks for the effectiveness of its descriptions, and the team with the highest marks wins.

**Sacramentals:** Be sure to focus on any obvious sacramentals which are popular in the school or local community.

***Related themes:*** Presence of Jesus; sacraments; stewardship. The issue of misusing or desecrating sacramentals may arise. This should be looked at in the context of stewardship, using God's gifts for the purposes for which they were intended.

## CHAPTER 28: THE PRESENCE OF JESUS

*Aims of Lesson 28*
1. To explain what the term 'presence' means.
2. To show that Jesus was present to the people he met during his life on earth.
3. To explain the ways in which Jesus is present to us today.

*Objectives of Lesson 29*
1. That students will explore their experience of being present to people, and of other people being present to them.
2. That students will give examples to show how people can be present to one another.
3. That students will indicate the ways in which Jesus showed that he was present to people, through their examination of the Gospel of Luke.
4. That students will be able to explain the different ways in which Jesus is present to his followers.

*Number of class periods required* 2

*Development of lesson*
1. Starter, questions, content and exercises (page 153).
2. Content and exercises (pages 154 and 155).

***Starter:*** Be aware of students from broken homes, or other similar circumstances. Although this story is sad, it is basically hopeful and for some students there may seem to be little hope in their situation. You may wish to refer to the fact that although loved ones may be far away (or dead) and there may be little or no prospect of seeing them soon, they can still be present to us.

***Alternative starter:*** You can give two examples of similar situations. In one, the people are present to each other, while in the other they are not present to each other. The following are possible examples:
1. A student comes home from school with great news: she/he has been made a member of the team (basketball, football or whatever is appropriate). No one in the family takes much notice of the news — they carry on getting the dinner, watching television, playing with the dog etc.
2. A student comes home with great news: a member of the family (parent, brother/sister, grandmother) sits down and listens to the news, is delighted, hugs the student (or slaps on the back if more appropriate) and starts to ask questions about what will be involved in membership etc.

***Related themes:*** Signs and symbols; sacraments; the person of Jesus.

## CHAPTER 29: RECONCILIATION

*Aims of Lesson 29*
1. To evaluate the students' present perception of the Sacrament of Reconciliation.
2. To revise the students' understanding of this sacrament as a celebration of reconciliation and forgiveness in the community.
3. To show that Jesus gave us the Sacrament of Reconciliation as a special opportunity to turn back to God, receive God's forgiveness and be reconciled to the rest of the Christian community.
4. To explain that Jesus is present to us through the Sacrament of Reconciliation.
5. To give guidelines for (a) preparing for the sacrament, (b) celebrating the sacrament.
6. To outline the three rites of reconciliation.

*Objectives of Lesson 29*
1. That students will explore their experience and understanding of the Sacrament of Reconciliation.
2. That they will explore their experience of being forgiven.
3. That they will re-examine the story of the Prodigal Son in the context of the Sacrament of Reconciliation.
4. That they will show, using examples, the value and significance of this sacrament in our lives.
5. That they will try to enrich their preparation for and celebration of the Sacrament of Reconciliation.

*Number of class periods required* 5

*Development of lesson*
1. Starter and group work.
2. Content and exercises (page 157), first block of content and exercises (page 158).
3. Second block of content (page 158), content and exercises (page 159), first block of content and exercises (page 160).
4. Celebrating the sacrament (pages 160 and 161) and the exercises (page 161).
5. The Rites of Reconciliation (pages 161 and 162) and exercises (page 163).

This is a very long chapter. If all of the content, exercises, reflection, action, song, prayer and the history of the Sacrament of Reconciliation are used then this chapter could easily involve two or three weeks' work. It is a vitally important area to cover well, and this means choosing with extreme care what to teach and when to teach it. It is more important to teach one aim well and really get through to a particular group of students than simply 'cover' all the material.

***Thematic approach:*** With this method, you present different sections of the chapter separately throughout the year, in the context of the main themes of the programme. For example, Lent would be an appropriate time to look at preparing for and celebrating the sacrament; or when the students have studied 'Meeting God' (Chapter 7), they might complete the questionnaire and group work in the chapter to evaluate the use they make of this important opportunity for receiving God's forgiveness. Other sections could be undertaken in the context of sin, broken relationships, reconciliation, the presence of Jesus, signs and symbols, and the Church community.

***Vary the stimulus:*** If a particular class would benefit from studying the chapter as a whole, then it is important to vary the approach used in dealing with different sections. For example, role-plays are good for exercise 2 (page 157). Preparing for the sacrament and celebrating it can be prayerfully reflected on in the oratory; the action (examination of conscience) can be incorporated into this oratory class, as can the reflection, song and prayer. In groups, students can examine the advantages and disadvantages of each of the three different rites of reconciliation in different circumstances; e.g. if someone had a serious problem which they needed to discuss with a priest in the context of the sacrament; if a plane-load of pilgrims was in danger of crashing, and a priest was on board; if a group of people (such as a class) wanted to celebrate their experiences of forgiveness and reconciliation together.

If the chapter is studied as a whole, then the timing should be appropriate — perhaps either Lent or Advent. Students should organise a reconciliation service to complete their work, and to celebrate it.

***Related themes:*** See above.

## CHAPTER 30: THE EUCHARIST

*Aims of Lesson 30*
1. To teach the concept of sacrifice.
2. To explain why the celebration of the Eucharist is a sacrifice.
3. To help students revise their knowledge and experience of the Eucharist as thanksgiving, praise and worship.
4. To revise the students' understanding of Eucharist as a sacred meal, in which Jesus gives himself to us in Holy Communion.
5. To explain that Jesus is really present in the Eucharist under the appearance of bread and wine.
6. To help students to prepare well to celebrate the Eucharist.

*Objectives of Lesson 30*
1. That students will understand and give examples of sacrifice.
2. That they will explain why the Eucharist is a sacrifice.
3. That they will explore their experience of celebrating the Eucharist, and give examples to show how their celebration can be full of thanksgiving and joy.

4. That students will be able to enrich their preparation for and celebration of the Eucharist.

*Number of class periods required* 3

*Development of lesson*
1. Starter, question, content (page 167), first block of content and exercise (page 168).
2. Second block of content (page 168), first block of content and exercise (page 169).
3. Second block of content (page 169), exercises, content and assignment (pages 170-71).

It is important to give students plenty of time to reflect on their own experience of the Eucharist, and to apply their new knowledge to that experience. Giving time to organise a meaningful celebration of the Eucharist is the most important way to teach this sacrament.

**Related themes:** The presence of Jesus; God's love and care; prayer, praise and worship; Jesus' death and resurrection; the Church community.

## CHAPTER 31: THE SACRAMENT OF THE SICK

*Aims of Lesson 31*
1. To show that people can need healing of different kinds.
2. To remind students of Jesus' mission of healing.
3. To explain that Jesus gave the Sacrament of the Sick to the Christian community so that it could continue his mission of healing, and so that Jesus could be present in a special way with the sick and suffering.
4. To explain that this sacrament gives hope and courage to the dying.

*Objectives of Lesson 31*
1. That students will explore their need for healing.
2. That students will give examples to show how they can continue Jesus' mission of healing in their own lives.
3. That students will examine the ways in which Jesus' presence healed people.
4. That students will identify ways in which the Sacrament of the Sick helps different people.

*Number of class periods required* 2

*Development of lesson*
1. Starter, questions, first block of content and exercises (page 176).
2. The rest of the chapter.

*Healing:* The emphasis in this chapter is on the healing aspect of the sacrament. It is important to give enough time to looking at the true meaning of healing, which leads to wholeness, as opposed to 'curing', meaning getting rid of disease. If possible, students should be present at a celebration of the sacrament, or a priest could be invited to speak with them about his experiences of this sacrament. Students should be encouraged to see themselves as 'healers' in their own life-situation.
*Related themes:* Suffering; death and eternal life; the presence of Jesus; God's love and care; the Church community; signs and symbols.

## UNIT VI: THE CHRISTIAN COMMUNITY
## CHAPTER 32: THE CHURCH — CALLED TO SERVE

*Aims of Lesson 32*
1. To show how a parish responds to the needs of the community.
2. To explain that love means service, and that this is our calling in the Christian community.
3. To explain what is meant by 'vocation'.

*Objectives of Lesson 32*
1. That students will explore their experience of parish life.
2. That they will give examples to show that love means service.
3. That they will identify needs in their local community, country and in the world and show how the Church community can and does respond to those needs.

*Number of class periods required* 3

*Development of lesson*
1. Group work.
2. Content (page 182), exercises and content (page 183).
3. The rest of the chapter.

*Parish:* The work on the parish community needs to be as real as possible. Give students plenty of opportunity to investigate and research what *really* happens in their parishes, and to compare it with what they *think* happens. They are often impressed by all that is going on behind the scenes.
*Mission/vocation:* If there are any returned 'missionaries' in the area, ask them to speak to the students. Ask different members of the parish to speak to the students about their work in terms of vocation. If possible, show videos and films about the work of Christians, both at home and abroad, who feel called to serve in a special way.
*Related themes:* Community; sacraments; relationships; stewardship; the presence of Jesus.

## CHAPTER 33: SOME CHRISTIAN DENOMINATIONS

*Aims of Lesson 33*
1. To show that Christians have a lot in common.
2. To show that love and respect for Christians of other denominations is an important part of following Jesus.
3. To give a brief account of the origins, main beliefs and practices of members of the Church of Ireland, the Methodist Church and the Presbyterian Church in Ireland.

*Objectives of Lesson 33*
1. That students will examine their understanding of the beliefs and practices of Christians of other denominations.
2. That they will indicate any questions they have about other Christians, and try to find out the answers.
3. That they will be able to explain the main similarities and differences between Roman Catholics and each of the other three denominations studied.

*Number of class periods required* 1-2

**Starter:** All of the statements are true. Students can discover this for themselves by searching through the rest of the chapter. Less able students can be given the correct answers by the teacher. They can then summarise what they have learned from the starter about each denomination. The teacher should decide whether they would be able to examine all three denominations, as presented in the chapter, in one or two lessons. If not, it might be wise to do one only, and come back to the others at a different stage in the programme.
**Project:** If you live in an area in which the students frequently meet (or could meet) Christians of other denominations, they might do a project (in groups) on what it is like to be a member of a particular denomination.
**Related themes:** Community; ecumenism.

## CHAPTER 34: THE ORTHODOX CHURCH

*Aim of Lesson 34*
To explain briefly the origins, beliefs and practices of Orthodox Christians.

*Objectives of Lesson 34*
1. That students will explore the similarities and differences between Orthodox Christians and Roman Catholics.
2. That students will be able to explain what an icon is and to give examples of icons.

*Number of class periods required* 1-2

***Orthodox Christians:*** It is good to stress the similarities between Roman Catholics and Orthodox Christians. If there are Orthodox Christians living in your area, you should invite them to speak to the class, or perhaps ask if they would be willing to be 'interviewed' by some of the students who will then report back to the class.

Many students find the Orthodox liturgical celebrations particularly interesting. If at all possible, students should visit an Orthodox Church, and perhaps take part in an ecumenical prayer-service. (This might perhaps be incorporated as part of a school trip or retreat.)
***Related themes:*** Community; sacraments; ecumenism; signs and symbols.

## CHAPTER 35: CHRISTIAN UNITY

*Aims of Lesson 35*
1. To show that unity and co-operation among Christians is an important goal.
2. To revise and extend students' understanding of ecumenism.
3. To revise the main barriers to unity.

*Objectives of Lesson 35*
1. That students will explore the need for unity and co-operation in everyday life.
2. That students will be able to explain, in their own words, the main barriers to Christian unity.
3. That students will give examples to show the part they can play in ecumenism.

*Number of class periods required* 2-3

*Development of lesson*
1. Starter.
2-3. The rest of the chapter.

***Ecumenism:*** It is useful to study this topic in a practical context — the plans for Christian unity week; a prayer-service for unity among Christians; or a meeting between Church leaders of different denominations which is reported by the media. Any of these give ecumenism a real meaning in the students' lives.

It is also salutary to note the problems caused in many societies, both today and in the past, by differences between Christians. This should lead to prayers for reconciliation and forgiveness.
***Idealism:*** Many students will feel, 'Why don't they just agree on everything and join into one religion?' This can be a difficult one to answer, given the students' lack of experience and knowledge. However, we can emphasise that it would be wrong for people to throw away sincerely held beliefs (conscience) just to give the illusion of

unity. Christian unity must be real, heart-felt. Wanting to be united is the first step. Students should be encouraged to include prayer for unity in their daily prayer.
***Related themes:*** Community; conscience; reconciliation.

## UNIT VII: THE LITURGICAL YEAR
## CHAPTER 36: ADVENT

*Aims of Lesson 36*
1. To show that Advent is a necessary time of preparation for Christmas.
2. To explain that during Advent we prepare to celebrate Jesus' birth, and his second coming at the end of time.

*Objectives of Lesson 36*
1. That students will explore their experience of needing to prepare.
2. That students will explain, using examples, how Advent prepares us for Christmas.
3. That they will plan to prepare well for the Christmas celebration both as a class and with their families.

*Number of class periods required* 1-2

***Advent preparations:*** We can take advantage of the media enthusiasm about Christmas to imbue our Advent liturgies with anticipation and happiness. Although advertising focuses on mere consumerism, we can learn a lot from its techniques and apply them to more worthwhile goals. So many 'shopping days' to Christmas can become 'preparation days', or a count-down to the big event. Planning menus can bring to mind the need to help the less well-off plan *their* menus. Many students in the class may be in poor financial circumstances, and it is essential to be sensitive if the class is planning to provide food hampers for a local organisation like the St Vincent de Paul Society. The story of the widow's mite is especially applicable here.
***Liturgical celebrations:*** Some prayer-service or liturgical event should be planned to mark each week of Advent. This is important to counteract the consumerism so prevalent in our society. These celebrations should be linked to the official celebrations, particularly the Sunday Eucharist.
***Related themes:*** Community; reconciliation; salvation history; prayer and worship.

## CHAPTER 37: CHRISTMAS

*Aims of Lesson 37*
1. To demonstrate that some customs encourage the celebration of the true meaning of Christmas, while others do not.
2. To explain the purpose and message of the Infancy narratives.

*Objectives of Lesson 37*
1. That students will explore their experience of Christmas, and note its significance in their lives.
2. That they will indicate those customs which help Christians to celebrate the true meaning of Christmas.
3. That they will examine the Infancy narrative in Luke, and see what message or meaning it has for their celebration of Christmas this year.

*Number of class periods required* 2-3

*Development of lesson*
1. Starter and group work.
2-3. The rest of the chapter.

**Christmas customs:** Other customs which are not mentioned may be used in your area, and these should be included as part of the work on customs.

**Christmas celebration:** Christmas is a great time for a class celebration, and should include a joyful liturgy, music and singing (dancing if possible!), food and relaxation. A lunch-time or after-school celebration is suggested, since a class period is very short.

**Related themes:** Jesus; the Gospels; reconciliation; community; prayer and worship; salvation history.

## CHAPTER 38: LENT

*Aims of Chapter 38*
1. To show the value and significance of fasting as a means of preparation and repentance.
2. To show that Lent is a time to concentrate especially on the most important things in life and that 'fasting' can help us to do this.
3. To show, through the story of Hosea and his wife, that people need special times to renew their relationship with God.
4. To give a brief account of the history of Lent, and how this history has formed our modern Lenten preparation.

*Objectives of Lesson 38*
1. That students will explore the Scripture background to fasting.
2. That students will understand and give examples of fasting as more than just doing without food.
3. That they will find a message or meaning for adolescents today in the story of Hosea.
4. That they will examine the significance of reconciliation as part of the Lenten preparation for Easter.

*Number of class periods required* 3

*Development of lesson*
1. Starter/group work.
2. Content and exercises (page 213), first block of content and exercises (page 214).
3. The rest of the chapter.

**Lent:** We present Lent as a penitential time, but in a positive and not a negative way. It is a time to recharge batteries and rekindle our enthusiasm. Like an athlete preparing for the big race — on a special diet, a strict exercise and training programme and a necessarily curtailed social life — the Christian uses Lent to prepare for Easter. The athlete experiences a special exhilaration in becoming physically and mentally fit in readiness for the time of testing. The Christian can also experience the exhilaration of becoming spiritually fit, improving relationships with God and with others, facing up to problem areas rather than ignoring them.

**Fasting:** Food is not the issue here. Fasting can mean giving up a bad habit, or doing a loving action on a *consistent* basis. Students should be encouraged to plan their Lenten preparation together, and put it into practice together. Each religion class might include a few minutes of quiet prayer and reflection, and a short passage from Scripture on the theme of Lenten preparation. For students of this age, an exciting and measurable goal is also useful to consider, for example, a 'copper' collection in a glass jar, symbol of denying ourselves luxuries, to be given to a particular organisation which helps people in need. Ensure that only copper, or small change, is collected, so that everyone can contribute, even the poorest, although contributions should be made anonymously if possible: do not let your right hand know what your left hand is doing!

Other activities might include lunch-time drama for the rest of the school, on the general theme of reconciliation, repentance and renewal, or posters on the same theme, changed regularly through the school etc.

**Related themes:** Sin and reconciliation; called by God; God's love and care; salvation history; Jesus' fasting in the wilderness; signs and symbols.

## CHAPTER 39: EASTER

*Aims of Lesson 39*
1. To organise and celebrate an adapted Seder meal, such as Jesus celebrated on the first Holy Thursday.
2. To explain the similarities and differences between the old and new Passover.
3. To explain the similarities and differences between the old and new Covenant.
4. To show that we celebrate Jesus' death and resurrection in the Eucharist.

5. To expand students' understanding of the Easter liturgical celebrations, from Holy Thursday to Easter Sunday.
6. To explain the significance of the Resurrection in the life of a Christian.

*Objectives of Lesson 39*
1. That students will celebrate an adapted Seder meal.
2. That students will explain briefly the similarities and differences between (a) the old and new Passover and (b) the old and new Covenant.
3. That they will be able to explain how the Eucharist is a celebration of Jesus' death and resurrection.
4. That students will explore the use of symbols in Easter liturgies.
5. That they will give examples to show how young people can show they are 'Easter people'.
6. That they will explore their experience of celebrating Easter.

*Number of class periods required* 4-5

*Development of lesson*
1. Preparation for adapted Seder celebration.
2. Celebration of adapted Seder meal.
3. Content and exercises (page 221), content and exercises (page 222).
4-5. The rest of the chapter.

**Seder celebration:** The outline presented here is intended to resemble the meal at which Jesus gave us the Eucharist. This is why Jesus' words of consecration are used in this Seder celebration, while they are not used in Jewish Seder celebrations.

**Content:** This is a long chapter, and the content must be carefully chosen to suit the needs and abilities of students. Some of the content should be covered before Easter, especially that referred to in aims 1 and 5. The rest of the content can be approached thematically, either before or after Easter. The new Passover and the new Covenant can be linked with the themes of Exodus and salvation history; the Eucharistic celebration of Jesus' death and resurrection can be taught in the context of Eucharist. The significance of the resurrection can be studied and explored in the context of Chapter 26 (Jesus' death and resurrection) and also linked to the theme of suffering.

**Related themes:** As above.

## CHAPTER 40: PENTECOST

*Aims of Lesson 40*
1. To show the effects of the presence of the Holy Spirit.
2. To explain what the symbols for the Holy Spirit tell us about the power and love of the Spirit.

3. To show that the Holy Spirit is present in the Christian community today.

*Objectives of Lesson 40*
1. That students will explore the experience which the first disciples had of receiving the Holy Spirit, and explain its significance.
2. That students will discover something of what the Scriptures tell us about the Holy Spirit.
3. That students will explore the symbols used for the Holy Spirit and explain their significance.
4. That they will examine their need for the Holy Spirit in their lives and in the life of the community.
5. That they will indicate ways in which the Holy Spirit is present in the life of the Christian community.

*Number of class periods required* 4

*Development of lesson*
1-2. Preparation and enactment of the Pentecost story; questions.
3. Content (page 229), content and exercises (page 230).
4. The rest of the chapter.

**Starter:** Less able students will need more time for preparation.
**Symbols of the Holy Spirit:** This is a very important part of the chapter. The Scripture exercises or the project could be used as alternative starters, depending on the interests and ability of the group.
**Assignment:** This could usefully be worked as part of many themes throughout the programme, e.g. Jesus' death and resurrection or the Christian community and vocation.
**Related themes:** Signs and symbols; sacraments; community; Jesus' death and resurrection; history of salvation.

## UNIT VIII: WORSHIP AND PRAYER
## CHAPTER 41: MARY

*Aims of Lesson 41*
1. To explain the main celebrations of Mary's life which are part of our liturgical year.
2. To show the significance of the events celebrated for Christians today.
3. To explain briefly the role of Mary in our salvation.

*Objectives of Lesson 41*
1. That students will be able to describe and explain the main feasts which celebrate Mary's life.
2. That they will be able to show the significance of the events in Mary's life for Christians today.
3. That students will explain what they can learn from Mary's example.

*Number of class periods required* 1-2

***Starter:*** Less able students will need direction and guidance to achieve success in this exercise. They should attempt it as a group. It is appropriate to give this exercise just before or after a school holiday, e.g. 8 December, the Immaculate Conception, so that students will have a very real context for their study. (Nothing is more real to students than a day off school!)
***Related themes:*** Community; relationships; suffering; vocation and service; signs and symbols.

## CHAPTER 42: PRAYER

*Aims of Lesson 42*
1. To show that prayer means intentionally sharing every aspect of our lives with God.
2. To explain the meaning and significance of worship.

*Objectives of Lesson 42*
1. That students will explore their experience of prayer and examine the contexts in which they pray.
2. That they will give examples showing how young people can worship God.

*Number of class periods required* 2

*Development of lesson*
1. Starter and group work.
2. The rest of the chapter.

***Starter:*** Other situations may be included as appropriate.
***Discussion:*** This should only be included if the class is reasonably mature and co-operative, since the subject matter is (or could be) quite personal.
***Related themes:*** Called by God; meeting God; the presence of Jesus; signs and symbols; relationships.

## CHAPTER 43: PRAYER IN THE LIFE OF JESUS

*Aims of Lesson 43*
1. To explain the meaning of the Our Father and its importance as the prayer taught to us by Jesus.
2. To show that Jesus was a person of prayer.

*Objectives of Lesson 43*
1. That students will explore the meaning of Luke 11:1-8 in the context of their experience of prayer.
2. That students will examine their pattern of prayer in the light of Jesus' teaching.

3. That they will give examples to show how we can learn from Jesus' example of prayer.

*Number of class periods required* 1

**Prayer:** Many students will reconsider the value of prayer because of the stress Jesus placed on it. Jesus is an important figure to many students. This chapter should be presented only when they have examined Jesus as a strong person of action (Chapters 24 to 26). When students are allowed to 'discover' the Jesus of the Gospels for themselves, they tend to be impressed. The focus in this chapter is that it is *Jesus* who calls *you* to pray, because prayer will make you strong.
**Related themes:** Jesus' life, death and resurrection; God's call; the community.